MORE FORT WILLIAM MEMORIES

Fort William
in the 1960s

MORE
FORT WILLIAM
MEMORIES

Produced by Fort William Community Council

First published 2004

Published by Fort William Community Council,
Fort William, Inverness-shire.

ISBN: 0-9548845-0-7

Typeset by
Spean Media Services, Spean Bridge

Printed and bound in Scotland by
Nevisprint, Fort William

Contents

Back – Thomas Wynne, Keith Gadsby.
Front – John Brown, Helen Dewar, Mary Bruce, Anna Symmers, Ian Kennedy, Patricia Jordan, Donald McGavin.

Foreword
Project Funded by the Lottery Heritage Fund

Over the years since the first book was published by Fort William Community Council, we have been asked on many occasions to 'do another one'. This we finally decided to do in September 2002. Our vision was for some photos, yes, but we wanted to do a lot more about people's feelings and what it was like to grow up in an age when everyone knew their neighbours, when wonderful new household gadgets were coming in for everyday use by everyone, and of course the advent of television and computers, and to travel abroad was just a dream.

It has been a much bigger undertaking than we had at first envisaged. From our initial Tea Dance held in Fraser's Café (that's now MacTavish's) in March 2003, when we had thought perhaps 70 to 80 people might turn up for a nostalgic afternoon, only to be really surprised when 172 people arrived. It was wonderful, and so many stories were to be told. Ian and Mary Kennedy and Jimmy Smith supplied music and the Community Council acknowledges their contribution to a memorable afternoon. Members of the Community Council took contact numbers and we tried to visit or speak to as many of those people as possible, over the next few months. Again, so that everyone had a chance to contribute, the Community Council members the following week visited Victoria Court, sheltered housing, and where we expected 20 or so residents we had more than 60 people turned up.

Our period is from the '40s to the late '70s. When TV was in its infancy. No microwaves. Few houses had telephones, and those that did took messages for their neighbours. Many houses still cooked with the coal fired ranges. We did have a wide variety of shops – which covered all our needs. This was our time – and it is our story – if we do not take this opportunity to tell it as it was – we might never have the chance again. You might think it's not worth repeating, but somewhere down the line our grandchildren (or their children) might ask what we did, how we managed. Everyone of you has had a story to tell, and we have tried to drop reminders so that you can recall those days gone by. We are glad we lived then, and have some sympathy for our young folk of today, who have so many material things, and yet who don't have the same freedom to enjoy the lifestyle we took for granted.

We are very grateful to all the people who took time to talk to us, and to those who allowed us to use their private photographs. Many stories told to us cannot be printed, (but they were fun to hear) and we can only hope that those we have selected will jog memories – if they do – tell your children and grandchildren and who knows, perhaps in another edition in the future – a fuller picture of life in An Gearasdan will emerge.

For those involved in the compilation and production of this book, it has been a fascinating experience. We have tried very hard to provide a factual and light-hearted view of life during our set period. Any errors can only be put down to human frailty – "Our memory plays tricks as we get older!" We have accepted all stories as they were told to us, but with the passage of time stories change on repeating and names are altered or forgotten. A list of acknowledgements is incorporated at the back of the book. We know it is not complete, there were just too many contributors to list everyone, but please be assured that all your help was greatly appreciated and without it – there would be no book! We hope you will enjoy our efforts. We acknowledge the help in gathering this material of Jimmy Ness, and of all our fellow Community Councillors, in particular, John Brown and Anna Symmers. Their help and encouragement helped through difficult times.

FORT WILLIAM COMMUNITY COUNCIL
Patricia (Wynne) Jordan, Chair.
Mary (Donaldson) Bruce, Secretary.

FORT WILLIAM IN WARTIME

The 1940s Remembered

Anti-aircraft gun on the ramparts of the Old Fort, with John Paterson

The war impinged on our lives slowly but surely, and on our doorstep the Territorial Army Drill Hall was extended and a new military cookhouse built right on Mary Street. In summertime the windows of the cookhouse were always open and the most delicious smells wafted out. This led to our considerable rapport with the army cooks who, when the soldiers' lunch was over would hand out to us, through the open window, portions of the mouth watering foods. Mary Street seemed always to be lined up with anti-aircraft guns of which we knew all the calibres as we did with the aircraft the guns were likely to be used against. The British Aluminium Factory, being the only reduction works in the country, was a prime target and therefore was ringed with Bofors and Lewis Gun emplacements. In addition, to create the impression that the factory was even more heavily defended than it was, there were many emplacements east of the Blar Mhor which contained only telegraph poles lined up to the sky. That period was punctuated by the blowing up of one of the Royal Navy Motor Launches in Loch Linnhe.

We watched the crash of a Spitfire on the lower slopes of Meall ant suidhe, and the ditching of a Wellington bomber also in Loch Linnhe. The latter, with a failed engine, descended into the water and then gradually sank, nose first, while the two crew members scrambled up the tail to be saved almost immediately by a boat. The Wellington was later recovered and lay for a while on Fort William Old Pier.

The war took away the older boys, one by one, to the Navy, the Army and the Air Force. They served their country, in many lands, with great heroism. Many did come home safely when it was all over, but sadly quite a large number did not. Their names are recorded for us all to remember on the War Memorial in the Parade – so near to the cattle bank, where we all had such fun. ✧

Ian Cameron, Kenny MacRaild and Ian MacLean

Hugh Cameron, DFC

Hugh was Dux of Fort William Secondary School in 1935/36 and was articled to Weir Solicitor, West End, Fort William with a view to attending university to become a member of the legal profession.

He volunteered to serve his country in 1938 when war was imminent, initially in the position of air gunner but was quickly promoted to pilot and was among the first group of British pilots sent to Canada for pilot training.

He became a Battle of Britain pilot defending the island of Malta and was awarded the Distinguished Flying Cross for

Photograph taken in December, 1938, of Flight Lieutenant Hugh Cameron, Distinguished Flying Cross, his father John Cameron (Macadoo), his brother Duncan (Plummie) and his sister Molly later married to William MacDonald, Onich. The family lived in Lundavra Road.

valour in battle. While standing in for a friend's tour of duty he was killed, dying at the age of 22 or 23 years. He is buried in the Military cemetery in Malta.

Hugh knew of his award before he died and after his death his father went to Buckingham Palace to collect his son's medal.

Hugh's brother, Duncan, joined the Royal Air Force and made it his career before retiring to Fort William. Hugh, who belonged to a long well established family in Lochaber, has many cousins living in Fort William. ✧

Back: George, Alistair, Robin Murphie
Front: Sam Anderson, Bill Murphie, Kenny Reece

Some miles from Fort William in a remote Part of Inverness-shire, screened by a row of trees, stands Inverlair Lodge. During the 1939–45 war this building quietly played an important part in the hostilities as a holding unit for British-trained agents who, it is believed, for one reason or another, proved to be unsuitable.

Inverlair Lodge

HOUSE OF SECRETS

James U. Thomson

About eighteen miles north of Fort William, in a remote and picturesque area of Inverness-shire, stands Inverlair Lodge.

During the 1939–45 war it was a military establishment, but shortly after hostilities ceased the army moved out and for the past thirty years the building has remained empty. Now, however, the Lodge will return to life, the British Aluminium Company are leasing the premises to Inverlair Lodge Committee for the purpose of trying out new approaches in school education.

Among those on the committee are Lord Kilbrandon, Lord Birsay, the Countess of Mar and Kellie, Mrs. Naomi Mitchison, and the Aberdeen educationalist, Mr. R. F. Mackenzie.

"It is the purpose of the Committee to use the Lodge as a world centre for educational inquiry and discussion," Mr. Mackenzie told me. "It will be a clearing house of ideas and also a place where these ideas are tried out in practice. For about 36 weeks of the year pupils will live at the Lodge, each group for a month at a time, and for the rest of the year the accommodation will be available for small conferences and also for individuals who would like to complete (against a background of this peaceful and historic landscape) research and creative work on which they are engaged."

The Committee believe that in the evenings these individual visitors, with widely different interests, will have a significant contribution to make to the discussions of people more closely engaged in school work.

Initially, it is believed, the most pressing area for inquiry is the education of pupils who have to stay on at school unwillingly until after their sixteenth birthday.

"When new ventures are outlined there is the danger that people will see them as falling into one or other of the categories with which they are already familiar," Mr. Mackenzie said. "It is therefore necessary to say that Inverlair is not intended to be another outdoor centre. Although it will make provision for mountaineering, canoeing, skiing and similar activities, Inverlair has a much wider educational concern."

A change to education from indoctrination ? – or what was it that went on during the war at Inverlair Lodge, reputed to be

several centuries old and probably a farmhouse before its conversion into a shooting lodge for wealthy Victorians ?

Why should the army have wanted this relatively small dwelling in such an isolated spot?

Even today there are people in the Fort William area who will tell you they "know just what went on at Inverlair". Their stories tell that top-ranking Germans were interrogated there and of the existence of secret rooms with barred windows-including the one where Hess was imprisoned after his dramatic flight from Germany!

What is certain is that if any one of those in the Fort William district knew the true story of the Lodge, he kept his own counsel. Even the Campbell brothers, who farmed close by and were most likely to know anything, were never heard to speak of it – and the last brother, Sandy, died some months ago.

Interest has been renewed in the story of Inverlair Lodge with the publication of George Markstein's novel "The Cooler" (Souvenir Press, £2.25) which has aroused speculation among reviewers. Did

Mr. Thomson with a wartime portrait painted by a German POW

British Intelligence have a unit at Inverlair, and if so, what took place there ?

One of the comparatively few people with any knowledge of the affair is an Edinburgh man, Mr Alexander Thomson, a survivor of the 1915 Gretna troop-train disaster, a Cameron Highlander in the last war and a retired Inspector with the Royal Scottish Society for the Prevention of Cruelty to Children. And for thirty years my father has kept his secret. Even as an inquisitive schoolboy I never thought to question why his mail went to a box number and not to a unit.

His introduction to this

detachment was most certainly casual and came about during the late summer of 1941 while he was serving with the Camerons in Inverness. The Commanding Officer wants to see you, he was told.

"Sergeant, there is an officer coming here tomorrow. He is carrying out interviews. You are included, so make sure you are available," was the mysterious message delivered by the C.O.

Next day, as arranged, a Major serving with the Intelligence Corps arrived and an informal conversation took place. It was, the Major explained, "a Staff job, a special job", and Sergeant Thomson was informed that he would be posted at a date to be arranged.

"It was rather a strange chat about nothing in particular. No mention was made regarding the nature of the 'job' nor even the location of the unit, but I asked no questions," my father told me.

Even the posting instructions were vague – merely to get to Spean Bridge and remain at the hotel where, the N.C.O. was told, he would be collected.

On arrival Sgt Thomson was delighted to see a small army vehicle outside the premises and quite naturally assumed it was for him. But, when an hour passed with no sign of the occupants, and he heavily laden with full kit on a warm afternoon, he went in search of the driver and found two sergeants in the hotel.

"Where are you stationed?" asked the enterprising Cameron.

"Why?" came the evasive reply.

"Are you here to collect me?" he asked next.

"Doubtful," was the next unhelpful comment.

"Then wherever you are going I am bloody well coming with you," retorted the tired and frustrated N.C.O., who, after all, had absolutely no idea where his phantom unit was located. By now his mind was working fast as he considered all possibilities. Who were these men ? Why are they so uncooperative ? Perhaps this was some sort of initiative test ?

The vehicle set off and in due course arrived at Achnacary, where the Commando men were in training!

But the organisation was not so inefficient as was first thought, and when one Sgt Thomson, A., Cameron Highlanders, was not at the Spean Bridge Hotel as arranged, the authorities quickly located him.

Inverlair Lodge, the Sergeant's correct destination, was, as he recalls it, a fairly large building with about nine bedrooms and other accommodation, situated about eighteen miles north-east of Fort William.

There was a small farm, and very little more in the way of habitation for miles around.

"When I arrived, I discovered that the staff was compact – a few Camerons and a small section from the Intelligence Corps, including the Commanding Officer who was a Major," I was told.

"At first the number of foreigners who were there in addition to the staff was limited, but gradually more and more arrived until eventually we had about twenty. They were the reason for the setting-up of this isolated unit. Some remained all the time I was there, but from time to time others would leave to . replaced by other 'bodies', as we referred to these people. I was never told who they were or what they were doing there, and I never asked."

"The Intelligence Corps men were friendly enough fellows, but their duties were never discussed; and strangely enough, these continentals, who represented practically every country in Europe, adopted a similar attitude, which indicated to me that they had undergone some sort of

The staff at Inverlair Lodge was composed of men from the Queen's Own Cameron Highlanders and Intelligence Corps. In this wartime photograph the men got together for an unofficial record of their stay at the Lodge. Sergeant Major Thomson is fourth from the right in the front row.

specialist training. After all, when troops get together there is nothing they like better than a good natter," my father continued.

In fact there is no doubt in his mind that these men were involved in some form of underground work, and for one reason or another the authorities saw fit to send them to Inverlair. When they arrived or departed it was always in the company of two Intelligence Corps men. "But what about these stories concerning barred windows?" I asked. Father laughed.

"There was not even a bar where the staff could get a drink," he said, 'far less on the windows; unless you count the vegetable store, and it was so damp there that even the potatoes went mouldy."

There was a twice-daily muster, but then that applied to most military establishments, and the doors were locked at night. But what wasn't, particularly in wartime? During the day these men were free to roam the hills.

Each Monday evening a liberty truck made the journey to Fort William, and all were free to go – as did the security staff! These men from the continent wore army uniform and looked no different from the tens of thousands of foreign troops who were stationed throughout Britain.

"Mark you," I was told, "you had to keep your wits about you. I remember one Saturday morning after parade, the C.O. casually asking me to write a report concerning all I knew about what happened at Inverlair. I gave the matter plenty of thought – but did nothing. Then about 4 p.m. he sent for the report."

"I can't write one, Sir," replied the Sergeant Major. (He had been promoted a short time before.)

"Why not?" he was asked firmly.

"I have never been told what goes on here," said Sergeant Major Thomson.

"Are you trying to insult my intelligence with such a remark?" asked the C.O. (a Major in the Intelligence Corps!).

"No, Sir, but I'll *tell* you what I *believe* this place is, but I will not commit it to paper."

The subject was never again raised.

Boredom was one of the biggest problems which had to be faced, and this was overcome in several ways; not least was the collection of fifteen tons of scrap which was sent to Glasgow to help the war effort.

Only one man disappeared from the Lodge during the period my father was at Inverlair.

"I was wakened about four one morning by a Dutchman who told me that his room-mate was missing. He was picked up six hours later in true Highland fashion. A worker on the hills spotted a soldier on his own, miles from anywhere, was suspicious, reported the matter, and the Dutchman was back at Inverlair! He was removed shortly afterwards."

Yes, there is no denying a strange army unit did operate in that beautiful but isolated area of Inverness-shire.

Did it harbour British-trained agents?

Almost certainly, yes. But it is equally true to say that it was not the type of establishment where one would meet the James Bond type of character, as some writers would like to believe.   ✧

Mrs Eve Hobbs after laying a wreath on Remembrance Day.
Local Dignitaries include Provost Mrs Murphie, Mrs MacNeill, and Donald (Danger) Cameron.

THOSE WERE THE DAYS IN VIEWFORTH
Part 1

Iain Abernethy

Formerly of 2 Viewforth Place

Virtually every An Gearasdan local lived at some time in Viewforth Place – or was related to somebody who did! So here's a repeat of Those Were The Days in Viewforth, first featured in the Highland News in 1964.

Just after the Second World War some seventeen families had their homes in Viewforth Place – the red brick and grey granite tenements, those well-built but drearily located dwellings in the centre of town.

Whoever was responsible for naming the two buildings certainly had a sense of humour.

For the view forth from the redbrick part of Viewforth was of the rear of Caledonian Buildings in the High Street, and of the rusty red corrugated iron rooftops of the backyard stores of Peter MacLennan's.

The tenants of the grey granite block were a shade luckier in that their kitchen windows looked out onto the washing-bedecked sward of the Caley Green, that semicircular grassy patch bounded by the Rocky Brae on one side and by the high thorn hedge of Brunachan on the other.

But their front vista was of the redbrick tenement!

And it was a vice-versa vista for the redbrick families in Nos 1–12!

By the late 1940s the combined offspring of the 16 happy homes totalled about 20 boys and less than a dozen girls.

This was a most gratifying ratio from the lads' point of view (changed days, now) as the 20 of them, aged from 8 to 14, made up the 'Viewforth Gang', a very select body which did not offer membership to the female element.

To join the gang everyone had to prove themselves.

Feats like climbing the highest tree in 'The Jungle' (as part of MacFarlane's Garden was affectionately known), shinning up rhone pipes onto the tenement roofs, and negotiating obstacles in 'The Dungeon' beneath the granite building were compulsory.

And candidates were subjected to some other intriguing initiative tests before they were finally accepted.

Due to the pressing fear and ultimate disgrace of being left out of everything, very few failed.

All the joys and delight of energetic youth were second nature to the Viewforth Gang.

Organised raids on the apple trees in the gardens of Royal Bank House, at one end of Viewforth, and the strawberry beds of

Earnisaig at the other, marathon football and shinty matches, fishing from the slip for cuddies and rockies, and inclusion in the Hallowe'en Bonfire preparations, were some of the main pastimes.

Of course all the boys had nicknames – which have remained with them till this day.

Thus, without knowing their first or second names, many locals came to recognise the shouts to the likes of Coatsie, Nick, Knocker, Dodo, Peelie, Fatbum, Biscuits, Bongers and Tupp'ny!

Their stamping ground stretched as far as the Cow Hill and the Rifle Range above the then Plantation (of trees), Balfour Beatty's Pier, reached at low tide, Ashburn Lane and the Town Park.

The Viewforth Gang was an essentially boisterous, high-spirited one.

Subjected to school desks for nine months of the year, its members made the most of their 4 o'clock freedom.

At that time the Playhouse Cinema ran a matinee-cum-afternoon screening.

And, oddly enough. children were allowed in free, if in the company of a parent.

Once released by the bell, and especially when the weather was wet, which was often, everyone would run the half mile to the picture house and, with a breathless "Ma muther's in!" to the ever-obliging manager, Mark Simpson, would be allowed through to the see last hour or so of the programme.

More often than not, of course, the 'muthers' weren't present at all – and Mark Simpson knew that!

During Trials Week in May, the Viewforth Gang would perch on the high walls alongside the Rocky Brae and noisily cheer the black-clad riders on their heavy BSAs, Nortons, Ariels, Royal Enfields, and Matchless machines – and in sidecars.

When the 'Six Days' ended it was the turn of the Viewforth Gang.

With a heavy rubber tyre purloined from Grant's, Fraser's, Dick's or MacIntyre's – and a foot-long stick to steer it, the members would tackle the Rocky – the Town Hall Brae – and the other Fort William sections of the trials course.

If a Viewforth trialist slipped and allowed his tyre to hurtle back down the Rocky and career across the High Street, endangering traffic and Robertson's and Reid's windows, he was promptly disqualified.

The winner of the Viewforth Trial usually received assorted trophies like broken knives and slings, marbles, and cigarette cards.

The piece de resistance was a huge ice-cream from Boni's, subscribed to at a penny a time by the entrants.

In later years the Gang graduated to competing on bicycles, with cigarette packet clickers wedged in the spokes of the back wheel to make a motorbike noise.

Louis Gordon did a roaring trade in repairs that week. ✧

The Rocky Brae

Frasers Café Staff.
Back – Peggy Chisholm, Moira Wynne, Sadie MacPherson,
Front – Georgie (Harkins) Thompson, Mr Challenger, Annie Carmichael.

THE DANCE BANDS

The Blue Stars! What images of youthful revelry these three small words conjure up! Dance halls crammed with bodies, girls down one side, boys down the other, except for couples who would congregate opposite the band, most of the gentlemen with refreshments on their person or stowed away somewhere safe.

The BLUE STARS

Margaret Muncie

First pub. in Lochaber Life

With the announcement of another dance, there would be an enthusiastic charge of testosterone over to the ladies' side, and in often wordless gestures the invitations to dance would be issued.

All the hit tunes would be played 'real loud' – but not to the deafening pitch of today's disco, dance or club music. You could still hear yourself and others speaking!

'Johnny was a great guy for electronics,' said Alec MacLeod,

Billy, Aeneas, Henry, Kenny, and Alec at the Town Hall in 1964

keyboard player with the band for its tenure at the top in Lochaber. 'Everything was 'miked up' from the start.'

Johnny Edwards, from the early '50s playing bass guitar, was the original in the band even before it became *The Blue Stars* in 1958, Alec and Atholl Soutar on guitar being the other two 'originals'. Soon after this, Henry Burns on drums was the next to join, followed by Lourie Peate on tenor saxophone and Wilma Rutherford on vocals.

This was the line-up for the next three to four years, with the band playing traditional dance music until the revolutionary phenomenon of Rock and Roll exploded on the international and the Highland scene!

The Blue Stars embraced the sound and rhythm of Rock and Roll. 'We played a lot of blues,' Alec told us. 'Chuck Berry was one performer we really liked.'

In the early '60s groups such as The Animals with Eric Burdon and their famous hit *The House of the Rising Sun*, and The Beatles with *Twist and Shout* were an inspiration to the band.

In 1962 Wilma left to get married, and Lourie Peate went off to Australia. Kenny MacKenzie and Kenny MacCallum, both on guitar, joined the line-up along with vocalist Jimmy 'Barrel' MacGillivray.

One of Barrel's favourites was *Oh Boy!* by Buddy Holly. The band were real stars in the local area, and indeed were treated to some 'star treatment'.

As well as the R 'n' R music being part of their repertoire, The Blue Stars continued to play for that essential part of dances in this part of the world – the Eightsome Reels and the Strip the Willows.

In addition to the Town Hall weekly dances playing to 700, and the village hall dances, there were also formal dinner-dances to cover.

Regular gigs in Mallaig or Roy Bridge, Hogmanay in Spean Bridge with buses laid on for those travelling from the Fort, were only some of the local venues for the popular band.

There was no problem with the half-bottles consumed on the premises when your coach was waiting outside to transport you home safely!

Oban, Inverness, Aviemore and Fort Augustus were some of the other regular destinations outside Lochaber.

One regular visit was to Kingussie on the Friday between Christmas and New Year, with the band promising themselves 'We'll never do this again!' as they drove through terrible weather, frozen landscapes and sub-zero temperatures.

Wilma's mother was in the habit of giving them a chocolate cake and marshmallows as a post-gig treat.

One year the temperature dropped so low at Kingussie that when they went out to the van they found that the cake and the marshmallows had frozen as hard as rocks, and were completely inedible!

'Never again!' they promised once more, but they enjoyed the Kingussie dances so much ('One of our favourites,' said Alec) that of course they went back the following year.

Latterly, after Johnny Edwards had hung up his guitar, and Kenny MacKenzie headed for Inverness, the band welcomed two new members to the line-up – Billy Grant (guitar) and Aeneas MacCallum (bass guitar).

In '64 and '65 the band entered several big talent competitions, pounding their way to victory in the Highland Beat championship in Inverness at the Empire Theatre.

As reported in the *Highland News* of the time: 'The 1,000 screaming teenagers who heard Fort William's sizzling sextet The Blue Stars on Monday could hardly have guessed that six years ago these barons of beat were a Scottish country dance band.'

In 1964 they won the Selecta Instrumental Cup, again in Inverness, and in an article headed *Cue for Screamers*, their reputation as a pop phenomenon was left in no doubt with the reporter enthusing: 'It's not often I find a dance band who can really get the teenagers screaming.'

In 1967, with nine years of performing in the Highlands, other events were intervening and the band eventually called it a day. Barrel went on to sing with Hecky and Belle, and Alec got married!

The band were a big phenomenon on the local popular and dance music scene in the '50s and '60s, bringing the beat of Rock 'n' Roll, blues and swing to electrify many an occasion, as well as playing the old dance tunes music for the reels and two-steps.

We who experienced the magic atmosphere of such evenings will never forget and still remember The Blue Stars with warmth and affection.

Alec, Henry and Barrel are planning an evening of convivial reminiscence in the very near future to remember the good old days when The Blue Stars were 'playing tonight'! ✧

From left: Athol, Wilma, Alec, Johnny, Henry and Lourie in the Masonic Hall at Banavie in 1960.

Dancing

Many of us learnt to dance in the Railway Club, which was where Nevisport car park is now. We watched and envied the footsteps of Joe & Jean Robson and Archie & Annie Carmichael, who had so much patience with us learners. Then, of course, who could forget K.K. Cameron's Friday and Saturday night dances. They were the highlight of our week. Girls on one side and boys on the other, and woe betide anyone who thought they could slip an alcoholic drink in when old Mrs. K.K. was on duty.

On a grander scale, there was always the winter program of Dances to look forward to – MacBrayne's Dance, the Post Office Dance, The B.A. Dance, The Farmers Ball, the Police Ball, the Shepherds Ball, the Railway Dance, the Licensed Trade Dance.

There were regular dances in the Town Hall, always well attended, and sometimes conflict between villages – who thought the Fort William boys were paying too much attention to the girls from the other villages (or vice versa).

The Bands we danced to

There were many over the years. And we have several shown in these pages.

Dave Gardiner's Band from the 40's.

Jimmy Donaldson's Band.
The Blue Stars.
Dickie Murray.
Hecky and Belle.
Shindig.
Fergie MacDonald's Band.
John Cameron and his Group.

So many to mention.

Grace & Colin Neilson, David & Jessie Dingwall, Will Adam, ???
Front – Bill Brotchie & Bob Michie.

The *Dave Gardiner Orchestra* playing in the Alex Hotel in the 1940s

The Sovereigns – Donnie, Hecky, Belle, Peter.

Lock, Stock & Barrel in Croit Anna Hotel in the 1970s.
Barrel, Belle, Hecky and Alan.

The Rebels rehearsing at the Road to the Isles Cafe in the early 1960s
Duncan Kennedy, Hecky Henderson, Findlay Taylor, Alec Shaw, David MacIntyre, Sandy MacPherson

When the Moon comes over the mountains

Margaret Muncie

The Saturday night dances in the old Fort William Town Hall, situated where the Tourist Office is now, were energetic and often electrifying events in the local social calendar.

In the late '50s, when rock and roll was first making itself known with such massive hits as 'Rock around the Clock' (the wake-up call of Rock music), the dancing and the music were at least as important as who was going to be there. No flashing disco lights then, but somehow the scene was dramatic enough with the live band tuning up and the hall filling up, slowly at first, then all of a sudden 'heaving' full, the girls doing some last minute titivating in the Ladies (out,

through the side door half-way down the hall).

A cavernous space with a balcony, the Town Hall undoubtedly had presence and character and it was a great shame that it burned down.

A special Saturday night dance was for the culmination of Trials Week, and it was a really shoulder to shoulder packed throng. One lad wasn't at all impressed when his dancing partner asked him politely, 'Are you here on holiday or up for the Trials?'

'I came in 2nd, actually,' he answered coldly but with dignity.

There was the occasional disagreement between dancers, but considering how much spirits

was being downed on the quiet by the gentlemen, it's surprising that actual fights were few and far between. Or perhaps Time has drawn a diplomatic curtain over such altercations?

The Braxi dances in Inverlochy were for many the crème de la crème with a wonderful 'bouncing' floor (again – is memory accurate?) where the dancers were given extra 'lift' as they enjoyed Quick-steps and the Twist.

Torlundy Hall, the old Spean Bridge Hall Roy Bridge Hall and the fabulous barbecues at the Shinty Field in Spean were all part of the dance scene then. Many a romance burgeoned on the Shinty Field at midnight with the Moon coming over the mountains and the tantalising aroma of what seemed to be a whole deer roasting on a giant spit.

Added on to all the rosy memories of youthful enjoyment at the local dances was the music – in the late '50s and early '60s we were really experiencing a true revolution in popular music although we didn't realise it at the time. We just loved it, were thrilled by it, and enjoyed every minute. ✧

Round Table Charity Pop Concert, 1966, in the old Town Hall, featuring *Group 6* (photo), *The Rebels*, *The Blue Stars*.
Band members, left to right: Richie MacMaster, Fraser Egan, Tommy Graham, Belle Morrison, Kate Reece, James MacKenzie.

Back – Ian Young, John MacInnes, Bill Brotchie, Archie MacLellan, Ron Nicolson, George Watt.
Front – Nan MacInnes, Grace Young, Nita Nicolson, Christine (Teenie) Watt.

Wm Low's staff dance

From left: George MacPhee, John MacDonald, Maybeth Black, Margaret MacLean, Margaret Kearney, Ian Lamont, John MacPherson, Donald MacMillan.

MacBrayne's staff night out

FORT WILLIAM PEOPLE

Pat and Jack Robertson, each in his own way, were very distinct characters, and there have been many stories over the years, as with Neil Cameron, who followed on from Pat and Jack.

Robertson's the Ironmongers, the minute you opened the door had a most distinctive smell. Wooden floors, nails, leather, polish, paraffin, soap bars, methylated spirits too, all blended together to give that familiar feeling. There were always cats about, who lived in the shop – their purpose to keep down the resident mice population among the animal feeds, and food for them was collected from Lachie Wynne's, the Butchers next door, every night…

Downstairs were the animal feeds and paraffin, and upstairs the China and Pram Department. It was the custom for grandparents to buy the pram for their first grandchild – usually putting a deposit on the mum-to-be's choice of pram – to be collected when baby safely arrived. It was considered bad luck or tempting fate to bring a pram into the house before baby appeared. And Robertson's stored the pram until needed.

Many mornings, some of the local traders would gather downstairs for a 'coffee' refreshment! And to discuss the affairs of the area, town and country, and the wider UK. A slower pace of life, and time for all.

Pat and Jack Robertson

Farmers and crofters (country customers!) used to order their requirements in the Spring and pay their accounts in October. Six-month accounts paid when harvest and stock sold in October. Someone from the shop used to travel all round the Lochaber area in the Spring taking orders, and later for Winter requirements.

Ex-employees in Robertson's reminisce how part of their job every morning was to sweep the High Street outside the shop, once a week (or oftener if needed), wash the same pavement, and clean the windows. In the winter snow and frost had to be cleared to allow customers access without the danger of slipping. Salt or sand was spread on icy areas.

One story – a young lady –let's call her Joan – went into the office to get change of a £5 note. But as she opened the office door it caused a draught and took the £5 note out of her hand into the open fire and up the chimney, burning. Everyone in the office just stood aghast – for £5 was a lot of money. Joan was alarmed at her future prospects here, but she stayed for many years to come, and through many more mishaps.

Pat Robertson had the 'occasional' habit of secreting a half-bottle of whisky on the premises for his personal use. As it became harder to find places that had not been discovered, on one occasion he put his 'stash' in the bottom of one of the prams stored on the top floor and awaiting collection. He happened to go up the stairs one afternoon to find this particular pram was missing. Panic! Where's the blue pram from upstairs? Oh, Mrs. So-and-so from Mallaig collected it a while ago, she's away to catch the 4pm train. Pat, who never put his arms through his coat, slung the coat around his shoulders and made his way like a bat along Middle Street to the Station, where he finally caught up with the Mallaig lady and retrieved his stash. Needless to say, that particular hiding place was of no further use.

On another occasion, Pat serving a lady who couldn't manage the stairs to the China Department and who wanted six white cups and saucers, away he went – brought down her cups and saucers – wrapped each one in newspaper, then tied them all up with brown paper and string, quoted the price and the lady says 'Oh, I want six tea plates too.' Pat's reply is not really printable, but those of you who remember him will know his outspoken manner. (And smile!).

Robertson's used to keep a stock of large treble hooks in the office, usually used in the illegal catching of salmon. They were asked for, and supplied, 'quietly'.

This type of store is no longer with us; everything now is pre-packed and throwaway. Sadly missed, but 'Happy Memories'. ✧

The Water Board
Jimmy Robertson

Many years ago, it was said of Mr Jimmy Robertson that he carried in his head the entire plan of the water system for Fort William. One of his work routines was apparently to open and, with a plumber's key, adjust a stop valve on Belford Road around the junction to Victoria Road. This operation took place every evening and was presumably to regulate the water pressure from day to night requirements.

When asked by one inquisitive local one day as to what he was doing – Mr Robertson advised that he was winding up the Town Hall Clock. ✧

JOCK

Graham Brooks

The year was 1965 and I remember walking along the High Street at 5 a.m. on a frosty February morning. A delicious aroma drifted down the lane from Fraser's Bakery. I would have to wait till pay day to bite into one of their hot custard buns. Passing O.B. Ross, the Shoe Shop, I stopped at the Post Office to glance up at the clock and check the time. Across the street. Mr Campbell was sorting out his papers in Cassells the Newsagents. He sold everything from toys to cigarette papers. Cars and vans could stop outside the shop without fear of blocking the street. There was no hustle and bustle in those days. People went about their business in a calm and leisurely way.

As I approached Monzie Square. a great bulk of a man strode towards me, dressed in flannels and a string vest. It was such a cold morning that Lundavra Brae had iced over and vehicles were coming down backwards, yet here was this giant of a man seemingly immune to the sub-zero temperature. At sixty-five years of age, Jock Petrie was still a formidable looking force and certainly not a person to bandy words with.

Jock was an incredible athlete in his day, a Highland Games champion, a Loch Linnhe Swimmer, and a Ben Nevis Runner. Having retired from the coal merchant business, Jock had started work as a milk driver with Bill Cargill's dairy. I was a milk boy on Jock's van and was enchanted by his amazing stories and feats of strength. Whilst he was working on the coal lorries he had a special shovel made which enabled him to fill a hundredweight bag with two scoops. During the War, Jock told me, when he was serving in the Home Guard, a German plane flew over the Sugarloaf where Jock was keeping watch. The plane was attempting to drop a bomb or two on the B.A. Factory. Jock went on to say that he emerged from the look-out shelter and fired off a dozen rounds.

"Did the German fire back at you, Jock?" I queried in an excited voice.

"No, Graham, the cheeky devil gave me a wave!"

On another occasion, when Jock was working for Balfour Beanie building the Loch Treig Dam, the foreman asked for a volunteer to dive into the frozen loch to retrieve some tools that had fallen into the water. The foreman announced that he would give the rest of the day to any man who would retrieve the tools. Dressed only in a pair of baggy underpants, Jock proceeded to break through the ice with his feet before taking the plunge. Unfortunately for Jock, there was no transport to take him back to Fort William early so he decided to make his own way home by sliding through the newly built pipeline, sitting on a shovel. When he emerged at the B.A., his backside had been severely burnt on the hot shovel. Another time, when I was delivering milk to a house down Achintore, an elderly woman appeared and queried, "Is that Jock Petrie driving that van?"

"Aye, that's Jock." I answered. She went on to remark that he was the only coalman she knew who could carry a bag of coal on each shoulder up to her bunker. What remarkable strength, I thought, especially since there were three flights of stairs to climb.

I suppose Jock was one of my boyhood heroes. Some of his tales may have been on the tall side, but I preferred to believe every word of them, Jock could not tolerate weakness in any man; he was a hard working honest person who loved a challenge. Indeed, when he reached the summit of the Ben during a race, he stopped to chat to a tourist. After a few minutes, the tourist mentioned to Jock that he was losing time. Jock gave him the answer: "Ach, man, I'm only doing this race for a bit of fun!"

When Jock Petrie passed away, Lochaber lost one of its greatest characters. Although I was only a boy and he an old man, he left me with life-long memories of days gone by.   ✧

Charles Dillon

Very few Fort William people during the second half of the 20th century did not receive the administrations of a major character in the dental surgery field. Charles Dillon is remembered by children and adults alike with fond memories of his unstinting devotion to the alleviation of dental pain and his sometimes amusing and eccentric methods of achieving this. Charlie , as he was known to one and all hailed from Kingston, Jamaica, where his father was the port doctor and he practised dentistry at his various homes in Fort William, after qualifying in the USA.

When keeping an appointment for treatment it was often wise to leave a reasonable margin of time, owing to Charles's predilection for cartoons. When asked whether one liked 'Tom and Jerry' – an answer in the affirmative was likely to bring a halt to treatment whilst the TV alongside his dental chair was switched on for a little light relief.

On attaining the age of seventy (still not retired), Charles took up mountain climbing and reached, over the years, a number of summits around Lochaber. The highlight of his mountain days was when two friends took him to the North Face of Ben Nevis and fitted him with crampons to ascend a portion of this difficult climb in true Alpine style.

He kept himself fit by doing press-ups and knee bends and survived after many adventures until his mid-nineties. He is sadly missed still.   ✧

Gus MacDonald

Angus John MacDonald, Gus as he was known was born on the 21st July 1911 in South Queensferry directly below the present Forth Rail Bridge. His father came from South Uist whilst his mother hailed from Donegal in Ireland, providing a good mixture of Gaelic cultures. His father worked in the coal mines of that area and when Gus left school at fifteen he joined his father underground in the mine. The 1926 Miners Strike meant that the family had to move in order to find work. This came in the form of a job at the British Aluminium factory in Kinlochleven.

Initially Gus's father walked from Queensferry to Kinlochleven to find this position and only after some money had been saved were the family able to follow. At that time they lived in a house in Foyers Road. Father and sons took whatever work they could find until they had scraped enough money together to buy a lorry which they employed to deliver anything and everything until they finally obtained a contract to supply coal to the Dam. This was not so simple as it seemed as the lorry could only go so far along the road before off-loading all the coal. At that point it was up to Gus to complete the two miles to the delivery point and this he did in an unusual way. He constructed a trailer like a sidecar, which he attached to his somewhat ramshackle bicycle, loaded it with five hundredweight of coal and set off to cover the last stage of the journey. This involved cycling along the top of the conduits with a frightening drop of 200 feet on one side. Needless to say this perilous journey had to be undertaken on many occasions to fulfil the contract. Yet to Gus this was all in a day's work and he thought little of the difficulty. Eventually he got a job in the carbon factory of the BA where conditions were such at that time, it was sometimes impossible to see the worker next to him even although he was a mere eight feet away. This was not at all good for the health all things considered but goggles, masks or breathing apparatus were of course unheard of at that time. It was merely the case that you did the job or somebody else would willingly take your place. Gus, as always, did the job.

In 1935 Gus met a young lady who was working for the Fairfax-Lucy family at Callart House. Her name was Margaret Jane Gibson. Peggy, as she was known, later went to work at the King's House in Glencoe. They courted for a while and were married in 1937, living in Kinlochleven where they started a family.

The onset of World War 2 saw Gus and many other young men of his generation, join the army. He was fortunate in that he survived which many of contemporaries did not. Always a good singer Gus had been invited to go with ENSA to entertain the troops and leave the hard grind of an ordinary soldier's life. Typically Gus felt this was not quite the thing to do and that he should stay with the boys and 'do his bit'. Perhaps if he had, things would have been different and a different type of career would have ensued. Yet it was not to be and Gus returned from the war to begin work again in the BA. Conditions there had not improved so Gus began to think that he would have to find a different lifestyle for the good of his health and the wellbeing of his family.

At that time, he heard of a small croft for sale in Blarmafoldach in Fort William which he viewed and bought in 1947, starting the long association of the MacDonald family with that area which still continues today. In the meantime the family grew. There was Angus, Margaret who sadly died at two months, the twins Norman and Patricia followed by Marion and Ronald, known as Guy, all of whom were born at Kinlochleven, followed finally by Colin the youngest who came into this world

at Blarmafoldach

Gus did various jobs as he was willing to try his hand at anything and nothing daunted him. He worked for the Hydro Board during the day and was a night porter at the Highland Hotel at the same time; in fact, he tackled anything which would help him support his family. Never shy of work, he was always trying to better himself and provide a better lifestyle for the family, which led from one moneymaking venture to another.

To some people he was known as Gus the Pigman as for a number of years he kept up to two hundred pigs at Blarmafoldach. It was a common sight in those days to see Gus with his Land Rover and caravan travelling all over the district selling pork which he had butchered himself. Indeed he was well known for the sausages he made which were reputed to be delicious. However, as times moved on, less pork was eaten as fashions changed and the business became less profitable. Undeterred, Gus started up a fish and chip van business, which was really successful for a number of years. Unfortunately, fish became scarcer

and potatoes rose dramatically in price making the business unsustainable. Nothing daunted Gus started a snack bar in which he made his own hamburgers. Many a Fort William worthy enjoyed his speciality of hamburger, cheese, with a fried egg on the top late at night in the Tweeddale Car Park. Again due to circumstances, his inability to obtain a permit and constantly being moved from pillar to post, led to the abandonment of that business.

He went to work for the Council Roads Department and could be seen throughout the area fulfilling the requirements of this task. Later he became a day porter in the Hospital where his highly developed sense of humour came in very handy indeed. On one occasion he dressed in full priest's outfit and went round the wards cheering up all the local patients some of whom were completely taken in by this disguise. This type of joke was typical of the man. He was indeed a true character finding time to laugh and joke with anyone and everyone. At one time the rumour flew around the Fort that he and Lachie MacDonald had struck gold in Blarmafoldach after a session of panning in the river. When questioned on the veracity of this report Gus told the questioner to look at the date on the newspaper. Needless to say it was April 1st. Hardly a year passed without a similar joke being played, such was the character of the man.

In later life he could often be seen in the High Street conversing with all and sundry. Some of his jokes might not be appreciated today, such as the time he stood outside Woolworth's cap in hand inviting a few coppers donation. When asked which particular cause he was supporting, back came the reply 'The road tax is due this month.'

Gus could never have been a successful businessman as he was a kind-hearted and generous person open to many a hard luck tale. He would always give to those in need and as long as there was sufficient left to care for the family he was well content. A true character, he found time for everyone and was well known and respected in the town where his storytelling was of such a quality that it was impossible to know whether the tale was fact or fiction. In a Fort William much smaller than it is today, he was known as a man who would keep his word, work hard at any task given to him, pay his debts, and look after family and friends.

A wonderful father, grandfather and great grandfather he is sorely missed. Yet we should not grieve over much as he was a man happy with his life and probably would not have changed it even if he could. Sadly, Gus died on November 3rd 1999 and Peggy died on January 30th 2002.   ✧

People – Where do you start?

Kate MacCulloch, Annie Curly, Jock Petrie, Paddy Heron, Jock Fraser, Peter MacCulloch, Freddie & his foxes.

Mrs. Eva Hobbs – she started the first Youth Club out at Happy Valley, she also did a great deal of work for the elderly. Not recognised for it today.

Johnny Moulvi, who wore a turban, and lived in rooms in Lundavra Road. He made the most marvellous curries, and quite often Dr MacDonald and Mr Campbell the surgeon were to be seen visiting for to sample one of Mr. Moulvi's curries. (No takeaways then!)

MacBrayne's Mail Bus drivers – Willie Downie, MacCallum. They took the mail to Kingussie to catch the mail train every night. and brought back the daily papers, which they dropped off to the shops

Gladys Aylward – tiny little person, who was a missionary.

Wendy Wood – When the Queens Own Cameron Highlanders received the Freedom of Fort William. In the '50s she burst out of the crowd and tried to pull down the Union Jack.

Dr Barbara Moore – first woman to walk from John o' Groats to Land's End.

This was our time – and it is our story – if we do not take this opportunity to tell it as it was – we might never have the chance again. You might think it's not worth repeating, but somewhere down the line our grandchildren (or their children) might ask what we did, how we managed, this we have tried to do.

Jimmy

Margaret Muncie

The fuchsias reminded me of Jimmy. She had a profusion of them in her beloved Canal cottage garden at Muirshearlich. On balmy summer evenings, after we had given Jimmy a lift up the canal bank from school, for sometimes she would have no transport of her own, we would sit out over coffee and a biscuit, enjoying her conversation and hospitality. A beautiful forest led from her back fence down to the incredible Banquo's Walk along the banks of the river Lochy.

If it was winter, the visit had an altogether different aspect, with the forest becoming a deep and dark place of mystery, through which any strangeness might be moving. (Jimmy had no such qualms regarding this isolation – on the contrary, she was familiar with it and loved it). She had no en-suite facilities – I mean, they were in an out-house, and when nature called, it entailed a visit outside into the blackness and rustling, and communion not only with nature, but with the now primeval forest.

Jimmy was from Dundee, but had made Lochaber her home. When we knew her, she had both the idyllic cottage on the canal bank, and also a wee house in Caol which was handy for commuting to the High School, where she was Head of Art. She had lodged initially with Mrs MacNeil, a Baillie on the Council, at 21 Lundavra Road, before she found her Canal cottage.

Life was never dull with Jimmy. Her nickname was an affectionate abbreviation from her christened Margaret Richmond Jamieson. A colleague on the staff said recently, 'Jimmy was very sharp intellectually. She could have been anything, she was multi-talented.' An inspired producer of Fort William Drama Club in the days of the annual SCDA Drama Festival in the old Town Hall, she brought sparkle and depth to the stage.

I first met her as a pupil in 1st year at Fort William Senior Secondary School on Achintore Road in the mid-fifties. A traditionalist in her teaching, Jimmy was always encouraging to all her pupils, whatever their ability. Her classes were enjoyable and relaxed, her philosophy of living permeating her attitude which was one and the same to her fellow-teachers as to her pupils. Jimmy was always a human being, never a remote tutor, or an irate tyrant, but with her striking appearance, erect carriage, and elegant appearance, invariably moved with dignity and authority.

'Angela' was painted on the side of her motor scooter, which she used to commute between Caol and Muirshearlich. 'Angela' was her affectionate name for her transport, which had, she recounted to us, not only taken her up and down the canal bank, but also over the Pyrenhees, and many a place in between. Some ignorant people thought this was her own name and thus she had a second nickname, Angela.

The unique (then) use of a scooter for a teacher and a woman at that, helped to mark her out as a character. But this was really a small part of her unconventional persona. Her forthright manner, her taste for a drop of the hard stuff, being the most colourful staff member appropriately enough, and by her own admission the inspiration of the song 'The Road to Dundee', made her a non-conformist well loved by all.

Encouraged and coached by her, I obtained my Higher Art, went on to Art College and eventually came back to teach alongside her at the new Lochaber High School in the mid-sixties.

There was no 'side' to Jimmy. When I became her colleague, I saw that she was just the same to me as when I was a pupil, she had treated us all as adults.

Her health was not always of the best, and latterly she would struggle into school although she might be feeling under the weather. She retired in 1972, receiving as one of her retirement presents a brand new bicycle, so she could still commute up and down the canal bank, 'Angela' and her three-wheeler having been consigned to the scrap-heap after long and adventurous service.

She was great friends with the other well-known characters on the teaching staff at that time, teachers whose names are remembered to this day with affection and sometimes awe. Bill Murphie, English, was one of her pals, being almost as flamboyant in behaviour and appearance as herself. Others included Wavy Davy – Donald

Macdonald, French; Poiken – Donald Macdonald, Geography, and latterly, young David Chalmers, French.

The staff picture of 1955 had a total staff complement, including Jeannette Macdonald, Secretary, and Bobby Beatson, Janitor, of just 20, compared to a total of '70 odd' at the present day. There was a family feeling in the school in those days when everyone knew everyone else.

In the early '80s, Jimmy began to fail, and eventually she had to leave her homes to stay at Invernevis House, the loss of her independence a grievous pain to her. Our mutual friend and colleague Judy Gadsden would take her out frequently for bar lunches, which I know Jimmy would have thoroughly enjoyed, and Judy faithfully visited her until she died in December, 1984.

She was unique, was Jimmy, and I have a lot to thank her for, perhaps more than any other teacher.

Her joie de vivre comes to mind when we pass her Canal cottage, her part of Caol, the Grand Hotel Bar, and of course, fuchsias.   ✧

Jim Rodger, Katie MacLean, Mrs Kearney, Donald Kearney, Mrs MacDougall, Fachie MacGillivray

Roddy the Tec

Roderick Fraser was a pioneer leader of mountain rescue on Ben Nevis and a distinguished policeman.

He was the first leader of mountain rescue on the Ben at a time when there was no sophisticated equipment or helicopter evacuation of casualties.

He once spent two days and a night on Ben Nevis, searching for and removing the body of an army officer who fell while descending one of the gullies.

His knowledge of the mountain at that time was unrivalled, and in 1957 he became the first member of the force to be awarded the BEM, for mountain rescue work. ✧

MacRae & Dick Garage Staff – mid '50s.
John Fraser (Inverlochy), Alistair Thomson (Corrour), Bobby Sandison, Gus MacDonald (Spean Hotel), Hughie Hunter (Lundavra), Roy Stewart (Arisaig).

MacBrayne's

Sister Shaw, Dr Connochie, Matron Reid

Mark Simpson and Willie Revie

THE RAILWAY AND THE FORT

Lord Abinger was given the honour in 1889, of cutting the first sod on the projected Railway line to Fort William. Some five years later after many amazing feats of engineering – some entirely novel – the first train steamed into town. The railway was to bring great benefits to Fort William and its people, but to their great chagrin the townspeople were to realise what a catastrophe it was in cutting the town of from the loch shores. However, it was done and about 70 years later – we made did exactly the same thing again.

Those who have realised, relatively recently, that the Fort was almost intact before the Railway required the site for coaling and watering berths, for engine sheds and for a turntable, are saddened to think what might have been – the Fort could have been preserved for information and tourist offices, for archives, library and museum.

The railway was possibly the largest employer in Fort William and it is only when one considers the variety of occupations that one realises why. At the station there were the station master, clerks, ticket officer staff, porters, signalmen. There were the Permanent Way staff, locomotive

A. MacCourt, D. MacLeod

men, steam drivers, firemen, cleaners, guards, shunters, coal yard men, fitters, joiners, painters, lorry drivers.

The engine drivers each had their own engines and liked them to be kept as spotless as it was possible for a working steam locomotive to be. In many families nearly all male members were railway workers and succeeding generations followed in their footsteps – in some cases as many as four generations. In some ways this caused the West Highland Line to be operated almost on a 'family' basis. In the 40s and 50s of the last century heavy snowstorms and long

Donald Kearney Snr and Tommy Wilson, Guard

The Age of Steam

Johnny Paterson and P. MacDiarmid

periods of hard frost were the norm for the winter months, and it is not surprising that as considerable sections of the track being at an elevation of around 1000 ft above sea level, substantial travelling difficulties were experienced. Snow sheds had been built to protect the line but in spite of this – blizzards and drifting snow could make the passage of steam engines extremely difficult and dangerous.

During periods of bad weather steam engines equipped with snow ploughs were sent out from Fort William to work on a semi-permanent basis to plough and break through snow drifts to keep the line open for passenger and freight trains. On the footplate and in addition to the driver and fireman would be a fitter, whose job it was to adjust the snow plough according to conditions encountered.

Sometimes the steam engines would require to charge into short drifts – almost up to funnel level – in an effort to break through and from time to time they would be stuck firmly in the snow. In really bad weather it has been known for four or more locomotives to be

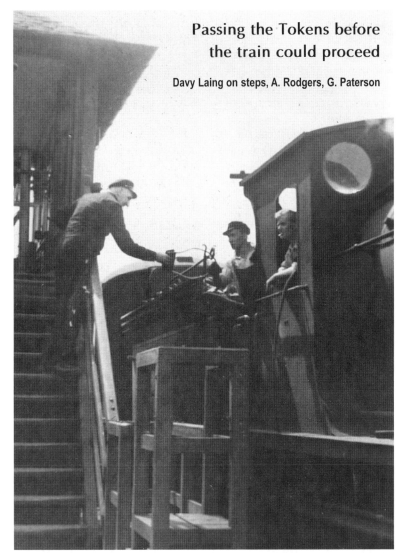

Passing the Tokens before the train could proceed

Davy Laing on steps, A. Rodgers, G. Paterson

trapped in the area between Tulloch and Tyndrum. When this happened the fireman would be required to make his way along the line to the nearest point of communication – to make a call for help from the permanent way inspector, Mr MacRaild and his band of gangers. Occasionally troops stationed in the area would also be called upon to dig the locomotives out from the heavy drifts. During one such event Mr MacLean (of Fraser's Café) sent out soup and other foodstuffs to sustain the diggers battling in ferocious conditions.

When bad weather was expected a single engine, fitted with a snow plough, would be sent out from Fort William to patrol the high and treacherously drift prone sections of the line.

It was on one such stormy night that a near tragedy occurred on Loch Treig side where the line carved from the hillside and some 100 feet or more above the loch was found to be deeply drifted. There was no way that Driver MacRaild could have known that one of the drifts he was charging into was, in fact, part of an avalanche which had cascaded down the mountainside and which contained among other debris – a very large rock. On impact, the eighty ton steam engine reared up and rolled over to hang precariously above Loch Treig. This terrifying situation was compounded by the fact that steam engines have a special plug in the roof of the firebox which allows an overheating boiler to douse the engine's coal fire in an emergency. Unfortunately with this engine being almost upside down, the lead vent in the plug melted and allowed high pressure steam to gush into the firebox and hence into the cab – almost blinding and scalding the crew of three. All three, Neil MacRaild, Donald Grant and another escaped with minor injuries, but remember that night among the most alarming of their lives. ✧

Standing: John Brown, Albert Timbrell, and others
Seated: Billy Corrigan, ? Cameron

The Railway Home Guard

They were a fine body of men, to say the least. Jock Brown, Guard was the 1st Lieutenant in charge of 'Dad's Army'. Jimmy Ross of O.B. Ross's Shoe Shop was the Drill Sergeant-in-charge. The drilling of this 'elite' band of soldiers was mainly carried between Platforms 1 and 2 at the Old Fort William Station.

John Brown, the Guard, was a King's Corporal in the WW1: a King's Corporal was a soldier promoted in battle. So he was keen to pass on his skill to the men in his charge. A lot of the training was done on the ramparts of the Old Fort, which was used at that time as Engine Sheds for the Steam Locomotives.

One Sunday Lieutenant Brown was going to show the correct way to throw a hand grenade. Unknown to him Jimmy Downie's boat was on the other side of the Fort wall, and of course, the hand grenade landed in it, and blew a large hole in the boat. The repair bill came to around £40 – a lot of money in those days. ✧

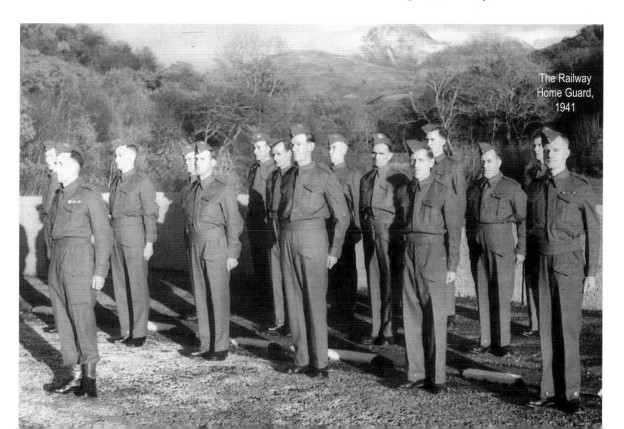

The Railway Home Guard, 1941

Nicknames of some Railwaymen at Fort William

Bob Sturgeon	*Big Bob*
John Allister	*Jakey*
John Cameron	*Macadoo*
James Paterson	*Soldier On*
George Paterson	*Wee Geordie*
George Clarkson	*Keechie*
Tommie MacMurdo	*Tammie Trout*
Angus MacPherson	*Look See*
Donald Kearney (Jnr)	*Toto*
Donald Sutherland	*The Duke*
Lachie MacGregor	*The Hielan'man*
Jim Rodger	*Handsome*
Jock MacPhee	*Jocka Fee*
Iain Gillies	*The Soup Cooler*
Allan MacDonald	*Allan the Doch*
James Gillies	*Skeesh*
Alex. Warren	*Gagsie*
Harry Sutherland	*Big Harry*
Archie MacDonald	*Stick Allowed*
Donald MacLeod	*The Hawk*
Jimmy MacDonald	*The Bandit*
David Keenan	*The Sugie*

Some of the other men had nicknames, but they were unprintable – or you just wouldn't dare!

The 'Pompers'

Many Railway stories are told of the exploits of the small Scammell lorries operated by the Goods Department of the Railway, known affectionately to the people of Fort William as 'Pompers' because of their rubber horns.

One such story is of a quiet (and wet) Wednesday afternoon, which was also half-day closing in the Fort. Getting no answer from Geddes the drapers, Archie MacLachlan, obliging as always, humped a large parcel of clothing around to the back of the premises, and left it on the doorstep, knowing it would be found there in the morning. It was found alright, by the Burgh dustcart, first thing in the morning, with the result that the parcel was eventually shifted to the An Aird Dump. Happily the resultant search following the inevitable post-mortem unearthed the goods – in a near pristine condition.

McALPINE'S FUSILIERS

As down the glen came McAlpine's men with their shovels slung behind them,
It was in the pub that they drank their sub or down in the spike you'll find them.
We sweated blood and we washed down mud with quarts and pints of beer,
But now we're on the road again with McAlpine's Fusiliers.

I stripped to the skin with Darky Finn down upon the Isle of Grain.
With Horseface Toole I learned the rule, no money if you stop for rain,
For McAlpine's god is a well filled hod with your shoulders cut to bits and seared
And woe to he who looks for tea with McAlpine's Fusilers.

I remember the day that the Bear O'Shea fell into a concrete stair.
What Horseface said, when he saw him dead, well it wasn't what the rich call prayers.
"I'm a navvy short" was his one retort that reached into my ears.
When the going is rough, well you must be tough with McAlpine's Fusiliers.

I've worked till the sweat near had me beat with Russian, Czech and Pole
At shuttering jams up in the hydro dams or underneath the Thames in a hole
I grafted hard and I got me cards and many a ganger's fist across me ears
If you pride your life, don't join, by Christ, with McAlpine's Fusiliers.

THOSE WERE THE DAYS IN VIEWFORTH
Part 2

Iain Abernethy
Formerly of 2 Viewforth Place

Shortly after the Scottish Six Days Motor Cycle Trials, the gang began, in the far-sightedness of exuberant youth, to make arrangements for Viewforth's Hallowe'en Bonfire.

Yes, as far back as May, the Viewforth Gang started to collect tyres from the local garages and crates and boxes and cardboard from the High Street shops.

Armed with axes and saws we set about denuding the surrounding woods.

Parents were obliged to preserve all newspapers and magazines for the big blaze.

Most of the fire fuel was stored under cover in the Dungeon, the enclosed vennel at the rear of the grey granite building.

This area was zealously and jealously guarded by the young residents of that quarter of Viewforth Place.

For a week prior to Hallowe'en the gang members took it in turns to keep a day and night vigil over the stockpile, for fear of raids by neighbouring gangs.

An extra-rigorous lookout was maintained at the Caley Green after all the materials were built up around the 20 feet high centre pole, two days prior to the event.

It was not unknown for jealous rivals to try to set the vast pile alight.

On Hallowe'en night the Viewforth parents undertook to counteract any sabotage plots by guarding the bonfire and allowing the boys to go out guising.

In colourful and often grotesque guise the gang did their rounds of Viewforth and a few High Street sweet shops and homes.

Returning home about 10pm, laden with fruit, boilings, bars of chocolate toffee and nuts and after ducking for apples at Provost George MacFarlane's open house, the boys prepared to light their fire.

The youngest member of the gang was given the privilege of setting the bonfire alight.

Meanwhile the bangers, rockets, Roman Candles and Catherine Wheels were going off in all directions.

Crowds gathered from all over town and close on 200 folk were known to watch the Viewforth Bonfire.

As a special treat the gang were allowed up until around midnight to marvel at their very own towering inferno.

Next morning everyone rushed back to the Caley Green to see if the fire was still burning. It usually was.

The culmination of the efforts came when the *Highland News* carried this news paragraph on the

Fort William page:

The Viewforth Bonfire (lit this year by George MacGeachie / Archie Pryce / Alistair Hunter) was once again the biggest Hallowe'en blaze and could be seen from all over town.

Soon after Hallowe'en (Guy Fawkes didn't have a look-in in those days) the Gang Hut season came in.

Because of the Fort's high rainfall a place of refuge was necessary, a dry, centrally located meeting point.

So it was back on the scrounge.

Corrugated iron (corry), old bedsteads, planks of wood, sacking and felt were purloined and collected from the most obscure sources.

As a rule the hut took the form of a lean-to, supported by a convenient wall, but the more superior, free-standing edifices on the Caley Green featured Tilley lamps and chimneys.

About this time of year, the Viewforth mums and not a few shopkeepers would be at a loss to explain the disappearance of considerable quantities of potatoes.

Had they snooped around the gang huts they would have seen that the tatties had found their way to the end of stout, sharpened sticks, and were being roasted over the fire.

Often the spuds were accompanied by black pudding rounds, passed under duress through the back shop gate of MacDonald and Forbes by a diminutive apprentice.

The roast potatoes invariably turned out blacker than the black puddings.

It was in the huts that most of the Viewforth Gang were initiated as members of the Smokers Union.

But by puffing at cinnamon sticks, instead of chewing at them, many of the boys were put off smoking for life.

It's an ill wind…   ✧

Some of the Viewforth Gang and the Community Council may be found in the photograph at the bottom of the page.

The Ben

A STROLL UP BEN NEVIS

Graham Brookes

It was the first Saturday in September. I was standing amongst a crowd of three hundred and fifty bodies and the smell of garlic and liniment was overpowering. The assortment of brightly coloured shorts and vests was bobbing about impatiently – it was the start of the Ben Nevis Race. My last race had been a cross-country affair when I was a schoolboy. Now at the age of thirty, although nervous, I was confident that I could run the Ben. As the starter's gun cracked, the runners sped out of the park and along the road to Achintee. This was where I made my first mistake. As I stopped to tie a shoe lace two dozen feet trampled me to the ground. I managed to roll into the sanctuary of the ditch. having regained my composure, I followed on behind a man with a long white beard, affectionately known as "Old Eddie". By the time I reached the mountain the pace had slowed dramatically, my nerves had gone but so had my lungs and legs. A lady with a pigtail trotted past. I felt a deep sense of shame. Then came a gent in his late fifties, remarking as he went, "You are doing well, lad".

My confidence was disappearing fast. I trudged wearily upwards amongst a long line of gasping breathless bodies. The leaders had long since disappeared. As we climbed up the steep scree slope, a thick mist descended. A runner called over apprehensively, "Which way?"

"Follow the man in front," I replied.

"But which man does the leader follow?" he answered. I had no more breath to deal with silly questions as I concentrated on climbing upwards.

An ashen faced runner spoke to me in a low voice, "Have we much further to go?"

ben nevis

graham brooks and john macrae

"Not long now," I lied. I had no idea where the summit was – never mind how far. But the poor wretch looked as if he needed some encouragement. Suddenly a runner appeared, hurtling downwards. The leaders had turned and were away on their way back. I did not know which way to dive, right or left, as runners descended straight at me out of the mist. A few minutes later, we emerged onto the plateau, a blue sky above. With my fears gone, new strength came into "my legs and I broke into a trot. As I passed Gardy Loo Gully, I heard a shout of encouragement, looked across and saw Willie Anderson perched at the edge of a thousand foot drop. I remember thinking that no sober man would possibly stand there like that. Willie was to stand there for the next ten Ben Nevis Races. As I approached the summit cairn, I put on a false smile and remarked to the marshals as casually as humanly possible, "Grand day for a stroll, lads."

I then turned and ran back down the mountain. As I descended the rough scree, runners were staggering in all directions, and the noise of the falling rocks above spurred me on even faster Then came the dreaded grassy slope, 800 feet of horrendous thigh pain or a green backside. I chose the latter.

At the bottom, a quick drink from the Red Burn and back onto the bridle path. As I neared the end of the mountain, I felt a great sense of joy until I reached the road at Achintee. My legs had turned to jelly and buckled. A passing runner shouted, "Keep going – only a mile left." Only a mile, I thought, why did he have to remind me. I have heard say that it takes an average man ten minutes to walk a mile, it took me eleven minutes to run one.

As I staggered round the park to the cheers of the crowd I heard a shout. "Watch your back!" A runner was attempting to out-sprint me in the last 50 yards. As he drew alongside, I looked at his learning mouth and haggard, pained features and hoped to God I did not look like that.

As I lay flat on my back after crossing the finishing line, someone shouted across, "How did you enjoy that run?" I closed my eyes and decided that the man was insane.   ✧

Glasgow Fair Saturday
The Ben Nevis Climb
Joyce Vickers

In the 50's and 60's it was customary at the start of the Glasgow Fair Holidays to climb Ben Nevis to see the sun rise. Then there were special trains bringing holiday makers from Glasgow north to the Highlands, and many came just for the weekend.

It seemed to be a ritual that after the Saturday night dances or when the Cinema films had finished, that folk made their way – on foot – from the Town centre all the way to Achintee and then 'up the Ben'.

No safety gear then – no helmets or boots – just the way we were all dressed after an evening dancing or at the cinema. All didn't make it, of course, but those of us who did along with our Glasgow visitors – we just kept going till we reached the top.

There we sang and blethered all night. Snogging went on and romances were made (or broken) as the case might be on these excursions. The lads often took off their jackets to wrap around their lass's shoulders. How gallant!

One occasion, Kye MacAskill was sent to get water to make the tea, while the other lads were building a fire for warmth. (It was usual for everyone to carry a small piece of wood up the Ben with them) Kye came back with a pail of snow, of course it was full of grit and 'fag ends' and the tea was awful – but who cared!

The toilet facilities were nil, but we all managed somehow, and as dawn broke we were rewarded by spectacular views (clouds permitting) before making our weary way down the mountain – to walk home to Annat – later to Caol. ✧

Glasgow Fair Saturday

Fort William Community Council asked so many people about their memories of the Ben Nevis Climb on Glasgow Fair Saturday. They just didn't feel able to write about it, but I list some of their comments here. Hope you recognise yourselves, folks.

- ☹ I wasn't that daft.
- ☹ I was drunk, I don't remember. (This was repeated by many!)
- ☹ I fell asleep at the Red Burn.
- ☹ My high heels twisted my ankle. And I didn't make it.
- ☹ I was wet and cold, and came home by myself.
- ☹ I only kept going till the booze was finished.
- ☺ It was a wonderful night, the company was good, and so was the Craic.
- ☺ Made friendships that have lasted over the years.
- ☺ The Glasgow folk were the friendliest folk we had ever met.
- ☹ My Mum wouldn't let me go.
- ☺ It was a great night, we sang every song we could think of, and 'Westering Home' (sung by 60 to 100 people on top of the mountain) still brings that memory back.
- ☹ The carryout was too heavy, so we partied at the wee lochan, and by the time we went to continue the climb, everyone else was coming down.
- ☹ By the time I was old enough to go, people just didn't do it any more.
- ☹ Too many people going abroad and it just died out.
- ☺ Great fun, the Glasgow folk really came to enjoy themselves.

Fort William Community Council – for the Millenium – had made enquiries about trying to do a 'one off' Saturday night climb. It was absolutely daunting. Police, Mountain Rescue, Medical Services and the absolute killer of the project – Insurance! We gave up!

Did we not know (or bother) about these things in the 50's and 60's.? or is it just a case of so many rules and regulations to abide by now. We did have so much more freedom! ✧

Eddie

Graham Brooks

We all knew Eddie Campbell, that familiar figure with the white beard and friendly face, who could be seen almost daily running along the footpaths of Fort William and Glen Nevis. Dressed in tee-shirt and shorts and clutching a handkerchief to mop his brow, this legendary Ben Nevis runner was an accepted part of everyday life in Lochaber. A modest man who lived life to the full and enjoyed the simple things that God gave him – his loving family and the fresh air and mountains. In recent years, he was affectionately known as "Old Eddie" but Eddie was never really old. When you spoke with him, you could see a sparkle in his eye and sense his tremendous energy.

Eddie did not look for fame or fortune and his forty-four Ben Nevis Races were not run for winner's glory, although he had tasted this three times when he was a young man. Indeed, even when he had reached the age of fifty, he was still breaking the two-hour barrier. At the annual Cow Hill Race Eddie would be standing on the summit every year. His words of encouragement, "Keep the trot going, boys," always seemed to give the runners that little bit extra incentive to keep going.

I once mentioned to Eddie that I had great difficulty in walking downstairs due to soreness in my legs after a particularly hard hill race. He offered me a simple remedy, "Try walking down backwards." It was also not uncommon to hear about local athletes bathing their feet in the salt waters of Loch Linnhe, a tip inherited from Eddie on how to cure blistered feet.

Eddie was not only a great athlete, he was also a great organizer and this was recognized by the Lochaber Sports Council when they presented him with the Service to Sport award, an accolade that was richly deserved.

Eddie Campbell's life revolved around the two things he loved most, his family and his running. His legendary achievements on Ben Nevis are unlikely to be equalled. In 1995, when Eddie ran into Claggan Park to finish his 44th Ben Nevis Race, the applause from the crowd was ten times greater than that for the winner.

Shortly after this year's Race [199?], I saw Eddie strolling along the banks of the River Nevis. He did not see me and I did not interrupt his solitude; he looked at peace beneath the mountain he had climbed so many times, the mountain that had given him a lifetime of pleasure. Each time I climb to the summit, I will see through the mist Eddie's white beard and friendly smile, and I will hear his words "Keep the trot going, Graham!"

Eddie Campbell was one of God's special people and he was special to all who knew him. Just as William Swan's name has been remembered for the last hundred years, so will Eddie Campbell's for the next hundred. ✧

Eddie is fourth from the left in the picture.

The Mountain Rescue Team

During the period immediately following the Second World War the greater availability of transport, both private and public, and increased leisure time allowed larger numbers of people from the south to seek the pleasures of outdoor life in the Highlands. With Ben Nevis on our doorstep and Glen Coe close by, the Fort William area saw a great and growing increase in the sport of mountaineering and, of course, the accidents arising from its attendant risks.

The new surgeon at the Belford Hospital, Mr Donald Duff, himself a mountaineer, became interested in mountain rescue and put considerable effort into designing new equipment, especially stretchers, for use in the field. Around him the local mountaineering club became very proficient at medical aid and recovery work and working closely with the local Police Force. The nucleus of the present Mountain Rescue Team came into being as the largest and among the most active teams in Britain.

The Team developed through the various stages of 'Shanks's Pony' to the use of helicopters, such as Whirlwind, Wessex, and Sea Kings – and from coloured flares to sophisticated radio communications. In the 1970s the team were presented with the Royal Humane Society's Medal for Bravery as a result of a very long lower on the North Face of Ben Nevis in winter. The medal, with citation, is now lodged in the West Highland Museum.

From left: Walter Liddell, Andy Nicol, Ian Sutherland, Terry Confield, Jimmy Ness, Tony Gaskell, James (Scooby) Paterson.

WORK AND WORK PLACES

As a young boy of 13 in the late '70s my first real job was working as a Hall Porter in the Grand Hotel. The general manager at this time (and for many years before and after!) was Mr Brotchie. The hotel was owned by the McLeods, Mr Alistair MacLeod and Mr Ronnie MacLeod.

There was a sort of open code for referring to the bosses: Mr Brochie was Mr B, Mr Alistair MacLeod was Mr A, Mr Ronnie MacLeod was Mr R and Mr MacLeod from Morar Hotel was Mr A Morar.

The Grand was a good place to work but it could be very busy and hectic for the porter, especially when a couple of coaches came in!

The system used for taking the guests cases to their rooms was as follows.

The porter would carry all the cases from the coach into the front foyer, Mr B would then check the name tag on the case with the room list and write the room number on the side of the case in chalk. The porter would then carry the cases to the required rooms.

A Grand Time

The system worked very well and was the best part of the porter's day, as you would usually get a tip from each room as you delivered their case. The worst part was that all the bedrooms were on the first and second floors and there was no lift!

This did get worse as for a few seasons the hotel used the rooms in the 'Annexe'. This was a series of bedrooms across the High Street, above the Top Shop which was also owned by the McLeods. It could be a real trial carrying the cases from the coach, up the front steps into the foyer only to find that you then had to carry them down the steps and across the High Street to the Annexe! And this was before the High Street was pedestrianised so you also had to dodge the traffic.

To begin with, I would take guests to their room, open the door and let them enter first. This quickly changed when one day I opened the door and the guests walked into the room and started laughing. "Do we have to share?" asked the gentleman upon seeing a couple already in bed! Fortunately all parties took the mistake in good humour.

There were some great characters to work with: Ronnie, who taught me the ropes as a porter, Dina on the dishes, Phamey as cook, Margaret in reception, Joan as assistant manager and the ladies down in the Cromag Bar, to name but a few.

My first Sunday shift got of to a disastrous start. Mr R always came into the Grand for tea and toast at 11am sharp and his tray was to be taken out to him immediately. Unfortunately no one had told me about this and the first I knew was when reception was demanding to know where his tray was!

Mr R could be a very imposing person, arriving in his white Rolls Royce, but he quickly realised that I had been dropped in it and he came through to the kitchen and showed me how to make up his morning order. I wonder how many businessmen of his standing today would take to time to help a lowly porter?

Two occasions that opened

HIGH STREET, FORT WILLIAM

my eyes to the levels of human endurance were Mod Week and also the time the Commandos arrived for a memorial service at Spean Bridge.

For Mod Week I observed first hand why the Mod is called 'the Whiskey Olympics'! Most of that week was spent constantly helping to restock the various bars in the hotel.

I thought that nothing could top that week until the Commandos came to town.

These were WW2 veterans who were up for a long weekend to attend a memorial service up at Spean Bridge. The level of hard drinking that weekend truly had to be seen to be believed, some were still going as we were serving breakfast! Their professionalism shone through the following day when it was time to attend the service – everyone was present and resplendent in turnout with honours proudly worn. These were people who fought hard and played hard.

My time at the Grand was overall a happy one. As time moves on some of these characters have passed on but are fondly remembered.   ✧

The Road Menders
by The Bard of Bogmonie
July 1972.

I looked at the Highland News one day
Where MacMillan has something to say
A Veterans Picture stands out bold
Combined their ages – three centuries old.

Four jolly lads – all guaranteed 'tough'
on litterbugs, and germs, Oh Boy, they are rough
sweeping before them the dust from the street
or keeping grass verges trim and neat.

First I'll take Sammy, the Wilson man
Namesake o' my own – the southern clan
He worked on the Railway for many a day
And a 'bob' for the Union he took from my pay.

Donald the Soldier – a real 'mountain man'
Climbed up the rocks to stalk the deer
You'll aye find him in cheery form,
With his good wife, in Tullochgorm.

Stalwart MacMillan – over six foot high
He worked on the track in day's gone bye,
Runner, Vaulter, Jumper too
Sport to the end – Hardy man Hugh.

Sturdy MacLeod, I have not met
Except on paper where he is well set
To carry all before his broom
And sweep all germs to their doom.

Slainte' to the lads – three centuries young
O'er eighty and seventy-sevens among
Long may they reign as 'Kings of the Road'
To them I write this true tale ode.

DAIRY DAYS

Graham Brooks

At the tender age of ten. I started work at MacLean's Dairy which was situated in Monzie Square. Mr MacLean the proprietor owned a fleet of milk vans of all shapes and sizes, the most reliable of these being a second hand furniture removal van that never seemed to break down. Each van had a team of milk boys who were responsible for delivering the bottles of milk to the customer's doorstep. Nearly every household in Lochaber had their milk delivered in this way.

I was a bit on the young side for milk boy status you had to be aged eleven – so I was given the job of feeding the empty bottles into a giant turntable washing machine. They would emerge from the other end of the line full of rich creamy milk, unlike the watered down versions they sell nowadays.

During the hard winter months when my hands near took frostbite, Mr MacLean would send me to the boiler room to warm up, and I remember well the Robin Redbreast who sat contentedly beside me. The waxed carton machine was operated by Aggie Russel who had immense strength and a heart of gold. I would run along to Cassels' paper shop for tea and sugar and Aggie would always reward me with a sticky bun from Fraser's Bakery.

When I came of age I was promoted to milk boy and was paid half a crown a week.

The summer months were wonderful – blue tits were forever pecking holes in the milk bottle tops to drink the cream and it was not unusual to meet a roe deer trotting down the Plantation Brae.

When making deliveries in Glen Nevis, I would search out a salmon which would be hidden in an empty milk churn for the return journey. Rabbit snares would be set along the garden fences and seagull eggs would be collected down Achintore Road, or the Golden Mile as it was called then.

The winter months were hard, and many of the diesel trucks would fail to start due to the hard frosts. However, when I arrived for my lessons at the High School my frozen hands soon got warmed up with the teacher's leather belt, for being late or falling asleep in class.

Dairy life was hard but it made us milk boys into tough young men. Indeed, it was four milk boys who dethroned the famous Gordonstoun team of cross-country runners on a dreich day at Portree.

Thirty years ago people were poor. I can remember one old lady who could only afford a half pint of milk every second day. She gave me a shilling at Christmas. I would leave her a pint of milk every day at no charge. Eventually my employer found out and informed me that there would be a difference in my pay packet.

There was – an *extra* half crown.

Many of the people I came into contact with have long since gone: Aggie Russel, Micky MacGuire, Bill Cargill, Dougie Edgar and Frank Gray – they all taught me something about life. Special mention to Ian Cameron, one of my favourite van drivers, a man who taught me honesty and courage, to never give up hope, and to Peter Hogg, who recently passed away. Peter always had a sweetie for me when I delivered his milk to Claggan Stores. Although a successful businessman, Peter never had any airs or graces, he was one of the ordinary folk who lived in an ordinary house in Claggan. A true gentleman and a grand fisherman who loved a Tales of the Riverbank story.

My only regret is that I did not spend more time in the company of these wonderful characters, but I suppose one does not appreciate the good old days until they are long gone. ✧

More Dairy Days
Ann Cargill

In the 1950s the High Street could boast five butcher's shops, three home baker's, five grocer's and several clothing and shoe shops, chemist's, tobacconist's and newsagent's. There were real ice cream shops and three dairies, all gone now. Our dairy was in premises now knocked down to create a better Fort William.

In 1966 we purchased the dairy business from Mr McLean and renamed it the Lochaber Dairy, operating out of premises in Monzie Square until 1987.

However, we had taken over not just a business but a family of workers dedicated to producing a quality product and delivering it to households and businesses, in prime condition and on time. In the back dairy there was Jack Brooks who guided our first faltering footsteps in processing. He was a big, strong Aberdonian who could lift two 10-gallon churns with ease. His knowledge was infinite, nowadays deserving of a first class honours in business management. He also interpreted the East Coast tanker drivers who to us seemed to speak a foreign language. One of these told us of an Elgin dairy that had been closed down because of "forky gollachs." These terrible creatures turned out to be earwigs!

The delivery drivers were Ian Migosh, Frank Schnozzle, Billy Brooks and Mickey Maguire. These stalwarts turned out faithfully seven days a week at 5 a.m. They knew all the foibles of their clients - where to put the bottle in a bucket with a lid so the geese didn't get at it, who needed milk for their porridge before 6 a.m., or to judge by the number of cars outside how many extra pints would be required.

Looking after the public in the dairy were Mrs Moe and Isobel and it could not have been in better hands. They saw to the collection of money and orders, and to the changes to orders and with never ending cheerfulness fielded the complaints.

Lastly, there was the army of milk boys who arrived like a bunch of chattering starlings at 5 a.m. in all weathers and ran from house to house, often challenging themselves to see how quietly it could be done. I am sure our lack of athletic talent to send to Athens has a lot to do with the disappearance of this hardy breed!

But what about the milk itself? Do you remember silver tops and red tops? Everybody wanted the more expensive red tops because of the head of cream – father liked it on his porridge. Then there was the infamous plastic sachet – a boon for storage problems but destined for a speedy demise when the milk boys discovered it wasn't necessary to enter each gate as it could be delivered by a judicious throw from the pavement when no one was looking. Needless to say, it did not always arrive in good order. Lots of complaints for Mrs Moe and Isobel! Strangely, the main complaint about this packaging was that there was no head of cream on the milk.

There was the occasional mystery such as the non-delivery

of the Sunday cream in Upper Achintore. One such customer was less than pleased, but the driver swore he had left it on the doorstep. Finally my husband stationed himself discreetly to watch events. The driver duly left the cream (justification for him) but five minutes later an Alsatian dog jumped the gate, carefully lifted the cream and ran off with his treat.

Life was full of ups and downs, the downs mostly due to the weather. Frost and snow brought frozen pipes, vans that wouldn't start and impassable roads. But the delivery done and a big breakfast awaiting on a good day could make Fort William a wonderful place to live.   ✧

The Ambulance Station in the Lochaber area was in Ex-Provost Grant's Garage, and the garage supplied designated drivers. Then it was run by MacRae & Dick on the same principle till it was taken over in 1973 by the Scottish Ambulance Service. When they took over they trained four staff. They were then based in Inverlochy and are still in the same building today, which was updated on the introduction of female staff. Now numbers have increased with approximately 15 doing the same work.

In 1973 they worked a 44-hour week and every second week you were on call at night – from your house. There were two 'on-call' drivers but sometimes when your partner was away 'You were on your own' and had to deal with emergencies and then you had to have neighbours to help with stretcher cases. At road accidents the Police or Fire Brigade would drive to allow the ambulance man to attend to the patient.

Mountain rescues always had plenty of people to help, but on one occasion when meeting up with the casualty – along comes Angus Grant, the Glen Ranger and left-handed fiddler who looked at our footwear and told us, for our own sakes and that of the patient, we should leave the stretcher and he organised eight well-clad mountaineers to take over stretcher duty, before we injured ourselves.

Meeting patients for the first time was always a challenge because they were worried about going to hospital, whether for check-ups or emergencies, and it was up to the driver to put them at their ease. This was sometimes done by a cassette of west coast music, allowing them to relax. (Fergie has that effect!) Invariably you could find a common bond. There is a saying "It is good to talk". How true we found this to be.

Drugs and glue-sniffing happened in the early years (and are still going on) causing problems for Ambulance crews, Nurses, and doctors, and eventually the police had to be called, with the inconvenience and cost to all that these services incurred.

Communications in the 70's was very much a 'hit or a miss' depending on where you were in the area and it was not until the late 80's that it improved when we used the mast above Treslaig and then on to a more modern system – where nowadays you cannot hide from 'Big Brother'.

When I started in Kinlochleven in 1969, patients would often have to use their own blankets and pillows, but thankfully this is now changed. Now we have defibrillators for monitoring heart rhythms and some drugs for life-saving skills. Ambulance men/women have to be so much more technical.

The changes in the last 35 years are tremendous and I hope that this continues, although even then, in the 70's, when they talked about changes – money always seemed to be a problem. ✧

Footnote – Alistair Grant, Alistair Fraser and Dougie MacPhail were the 'well-kent faces of our Ambulance Service, known and trusted by generations of the people of An Gearasdan.

Ambulance Memories
Dougie MacPhail

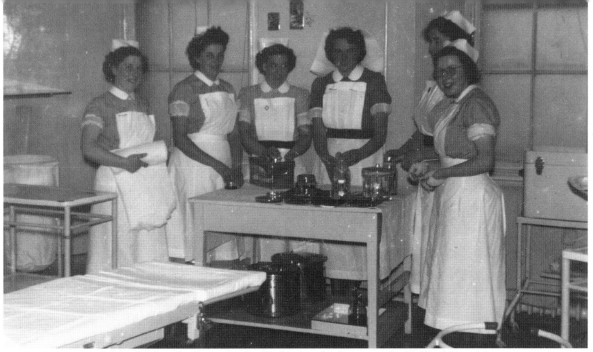

Mary, Maimmie, Jean, Annie, Katie, Ann in theatre at the Belford Hospial

Belford Stories
From the Old to the New
Cathy MacKenzie / Maryann MacInnes

First and foremost is the memory of a very friendly and happy 'old' Belford where everyone worked for the patients. There was a lot of strenuous, physical work but there was a lot of fun too. There were 36 – 40 Surgical, Medical, and on occasions Maternity patients accommodated in four rooms up a winding stair and also in a ward downstairs. There was no lift, so patients (conscious and unconscious – heavy and lightweights) were carried on stretchers, by the nurses, up to the wards and down to the X-ray Dept. 'Making up beds' had a different meaning there – as with a flickering torch and by the light of the moon, we had to go outside to an unlit shed and collect the relevant pieces, hammer them together and carry the bed upstairs. Fortunately the patients were unaware that the beds they were lying on had been put together by a young staff nurse and an even younger nursing auxiliary who had no training for such work.

We were glad we did not have any of that to do in the new Belford Hospital. Here the patients are accommodated on the ground floor, we have wide corridors, space between the beds and no longer do we have to run with the screens on wheels. Everything was brand new with modern beds and equipment and some new staff. The meals come on a trolley instead of pulling up a heavy hoist with a rope. Central Sterilising Dept. has replaced the need for us to pack dressing drums and send them by bus or ambulance to Inverness for sterilising. Each ward has its own cupboard for patients clothes – we had to carry cases and heavy climbers gear, in all weathers, to a cupboard in the Physiotherapy Dept. outside the old hospital. The Mortuary was also outside and patients' remains were carried on a stretcher down the stairs and outside, in all kinds of weather.

Now there is a night porter – gone are the nights when we answered the doorbell with trepidation (and with the poker under the cardigan). The old hospital attracted some unsavoury types, as does the new hospital.

Staffing levels changed overnight – in the old hospital there was one staff nurse and one nursing auxiliary on night duty to care for up to 40 patients, attend to casualties, and to prepare theatre when required. In the new hospital staff are employed to work in Surgical, Medical or Maternity Wards, Outpatient Dept. or Theatre – in the old hospital there was only one team. What we did miss when we moved to the new hospital was the 'esprit de corps' of the old hospital.   ✧

Major Alert

One evening Sister Pat was summoned round to the front door, as there were a large number of 'casualties' there requiring oxygen. She called on staff from all wards to come round to help The casualties were a tank full of fish en route to Lochailort Fish Farm and they were running out of oxygen. Sister Pat hooked up another cylinder and could have sworn the fish were smiling as they were driven off to continue on their journey. On coming back to the ward, Sister Pat was heard to say 'If a couple of stags arrive with their antlers locked – I am not in!!'

✧

A Slight Misunderstanding

The ward Sister had been told to expect a Romanian lorry driver to come at the weekend to collect the old X-ray machine, and he duly arrived on a Sunday morning – it transpired that he had no English but Mary was able to understand that he had slept in his lorry overnight and he hadn't had anything to eat – so it was arranged for him to have breakfast and Sister went round to tell him. As one does when speaking to someone who cannot speak the lingo – she raised her voice a few octaves and gesticulated with the hands and arms. The response, in perfect English was 'I don't know who you think I am, but I am a Minister from the Church of God.' Red-faced, she suddenly espied the lorry driver appearing – You couldn't mistake him for he wore a huge Cossack hat!

✧

The Telephone Exchange

The Telephone Exchange was first run by Mrs Grant from her home in the High Street, then as it 'grew' it was taken over by her daughter Elma and it then moved to bigger premises further along the High Street, opposite the Ben Nevis Bar (Hotel), shared with the Post Office.

There were usually 8 or 9 girls working during the day and some men working evenings and nights. Starting and finishing times were most peculiar; you very rarely started or finished 'on the hour'. It was always two or three minutes before or after the hour. Don't know why!

Miss Grant was, as most bosses were in those days, strict but fair. She was very conscious of our 'persona' always telling the girls to sit up straight, not to cross our legs, and to put a smile in our voices when answering calls. We were always conscious of Supervisors sitting behind the telephonists.

Saturdays were the best days, especially as there were no supervisors on duty, and only two girls. We would take 'breaks' when we liked, usually at the switchboard – a very definite 'no no' during the week. Plus one of us would usually run out to the Co-op Bakery nearby for the creamiest cakes we could find. Our supervisors would have a fit at such goings on.

Number, please!

Telephone boxes have always had a fascination for children. When answering a call –

- Number, please?
  Is that the operator on the line?
  Yes. *You'd better get off – there's a train coming!!*

- *Can I speak to Mr. Busby?* (At the time Busby was BT mascot).
- And on many occasions, when you asked 'Number please?' you were told to *B... Off!!!!*

Some of these 'little darlings' are now some of our most respected citizens!

The A and B button boxes were a trial, for you could never be sure when you were being conned, but you weren't allowed to tell callers they were chancing their luck when they complained *'I lost my money'*.

One operator who seemed to be picking up all these calls one afternoon, decided the next caller wasn't getting connected without her hearing the money going in. When the caller said the box just wouldn't take the money – he was told to go to another box. Only problem was he was calling from the middle of Glencoe – only box for miles.

Telephone Operators were also required to occasionally work at other exchanges, i.e. Mallaig or Strontian. Whereas in Fort William we worked with lights, in Strontian it was an 'eyeball' exchange.

One operators first experience of Strontian was arriving in the exchange for the first time to see all these 'eyeballs' dropping, and the very first call picked up was a very irate gentleman who said his wife had been waiting on another line for 20 minutes and why was his call answered before hers? No reply!!! ✧

Mr Jolly's Farewell Do, 1960: Betty MacDougall, Joan Steel, Anna May Shaw, Nellie Hayes, Dorothy Buchanan, Cathy (Riach) MacDonald, Margaret MacKinnon, Cathy (Clark) Stewart.

The Bus Conductresses

Cathie (MacDonald) MacLean, Margaret Kearney, Ena (MacDonald) Morrison, Joan (MacDonald) MacLeod.

Back: Janet (MacKenzie) MacLeod, Mr Brown, Mrs Wallace, Mrs Fraser,
Front: ??????, Margaret MacLean, Mrs Drummond, Grace MacKinnon.

John Menzies staff

Starting working with the Wynne Family Butchers in 1961 – as a butcher, van man, and shop assistant. The butcher's van went round the town area on Mondays, Thursdays and Saturdays, and on Tuesdays went to Onich and North Ballachulish. The van carried a variety of butcher meat plus 'bones for the dogs', and it was not too long before every dog in the area knew the sound of my van, and alerted their owners. My customers then would be ready and waiting. Joan Campbell's dog 'Crackers' always met the van with his tail wagging – and at Christmas-time I used to get gifts from my doggy friends.

The Butcher's shop was between The Volunteer Arms and Peter Robertson's, Ironmongers. Pat & Jack Robertson and Neilie Cameron were great characters. Never a dull moment there.

In those days, the meat was always hung on hooks on bars in the front shop, and sawdust was allowed on the floor to catch the blood and small cuttings. (Not allowed today with all the hygiene laws.) Any meat that fell on the sawdust went in the bin.

Then beef came from the local slaughterhouse and from a Glasgow firm. The local carcases were delivered by the Railways 'Iron Horses'. The drivers were Arthur MacCourt, Geordie Reid, and Archie MacLachlan. Always a bit of Craic with them. Summer times were really busy, really early mornings and late nights. We had fun with tourists asking about haggis and black puddings, and kept them going with the usual stories about haggis having long legs one side and short legs the other, making it easier for the haggis to run round the hills.

Boni's Restaurant was always busy, and at lunchtime if the queues were long – the restaurant was closed until the diners were finished and tables mad ready for the lot The weekend always had us making up dozens of 8oz. Steaks for Boni's Restaurant.

When a young chap started in the butchers, it was the usual tricks to send them to Robertson's the Ironmongers, for a 'long stand' or to Sydie's the Painters for a tin of 'tartan paint'.

Christmas time was hectic as we did a lot of poultry, killing,

WYNNE THE BUTCHER'S

Pat Kane

plucking and dressing, as well as the meat – beef, lamb, pork and venison, all had to be prepared by hand.

There were five Butchers shops in the Town area then, and all worked well with one another. If one butcher was short of something – they would borrow from another butcher and return it when they got their own supply in.   ✧

Memories of 76 High Street

Lots of people will have memories of 76 High Street, from Kyle to Kinlochleven and from Fort William to Mallaig and all places in between. Why? 76 High Street was for many years a retail Furnishers and Outfitters Store which went under the names of Rex's, Sloan's, and Black & Campbell at one time or another.

Mark McCann came to this store as relief manager in 1959/60 to cover while the manager, Cecil MacGillivary, was off ill. Cecil then decided to start his own business, and Mark took the post of manager.

The store had a staff of well-known locals over the years. The agents who covered the various areas were known as Sales/Collectors, and these included Don MacGillivary, Kenny MacRaild, Hamish Henderson, Bill Steel, Alistair MacPhee, Dougie MacCallum, Albert Burns, Alec MacLennan. Inside staff included shop and office workers Yvonne Tutty, Ian MacLeod, Jessie MacDonald, Beryl Edgar, Violet MacLeod, Walter Whitehead, Walter Liddle, Grace Brookes, and many others. Also included in staff was Kitty McCann who was Stock Supervisor. What is memorable is the friendship and camaraderie that existed and the way that everyone took such an interest in their work – inside staff and out.

Many people called in for a browse around the shop and a blether. The shop before becoming a 'Sloan's' shop was a working man's clothing store, and was situated between Johnny Gordon's Fish Shop (now a clothing shop) and Faccenda's (now the Granite House).

There was living accommodation above the shop for the manager. The flat was spacious, but haunted! I refer to No. 76 as being haunted, and this is absolutely true as we experienced many strange happenings during our time there, plus a seventh son of a seventh son traveller spoke of his experience when he visited the shop after it had been renovated – and he was able to feel a presence and tell of how the building had been before the fire. The fire happened in 1966, in the shop, but it gutted the premises. (By this time the premises were no longer used as a home – the manager and family having moved to a new house in the Plantation). A lady from Caol, 'Blondie' MacDonald, never without her Scots Terrier, wouldn't believe the top flat was haunted till her dog refused to go upstairs with her.

Mark McCann himself has had the experience of seeing, on the premises, the shape of a ghostly bearded man. (Staff called the ghost Fred.) According to the late Johnny Gordon, Fishmonger, the ghost had been 'accidentally' shot by his own wife. They had kept hens out the back, and when she tried to shoot a rat, she had shot her husband instead.

Since the building at No. 76 (now Toymaster) is said to be one of the oldest buildings on the street, who knows what tales it could tell. Visiting officials to

Sloan's would stay in only once on their own. At lunch-time when the shop was closed, they could hear shuffling and stamping footsteps, and this could be confirmed by Mr McCann. Despite all of this, it was a great place to work and live, and bring up a family. ✧

Back: Kenny MacRaild, Albert Burns, Bill Steel, Don MacGillivray
Front: Violet Macleod, Margaret (Redpath) Livingstone, Mark McCann, Jessie MacDonald, Beryl Edgar.
Photograph is of an 'Efficiency Cup' won by the staff 3 years running, and after the third year they were told to keep it.

Staff at the Alexandra Hotel

THOSE WERE THE DAYS IN VIEWFORTH
Part 3

Iain Abernethy
Formerly of 2 Viewforth Place

Half a century ago members of the Viewforth Gang delighted in watching the Burgh workmen baling salvage – scrap paper.

The work was carried out in the building, long since demolished, known affectionately as the 'Lemonade Store'.

This crumbling edifice alongside the Rocky was infested with rats and the Burgh men had some highly interesting methods of hastening their demise.

Over the years members of the Viewforth Gang dug up every inch of the ground outside the Lemonade Store and collected dozens of glass 'marbles' for their pains.

In a previous existence these had been the stoppers for the bottles of the aerated waters manufactured by Munro and by MacFarlane.

Digging, indeed, formed a vital part of gang life.

Boxes of spent cartridges (gathered from the Rifle Range on the Cow Hill) were buried at various locations in the Jungle – mainly so that the gang got some practice in using borrowed picks and spades.

These were about the only opportunities the members had for spadework – as Viewforth boasted very little in the way of garden ground.

After the daily miseries of school, group games like rounders, follow-my-leader and skeep were the order of the latter part of the day back home in Viewforth.

But these were commenced only after everyone had changed into their "playing clothes" and met "out the Front".

The "Front" was the puddle-ridden, small-stone-strewn, earthen quadrangle which separated the tenements.

Nowadays Donnie Corbett parks his van in the Viewforth Car Park at a spot close to where Dodo MacLean's jacket used to be one of the goalposts for Viewforth Gang shinty and football matches.

For these and other sporting activities like cricket the "Front" was cleared of dustbins, prams, toys, the odd bike and any other sundry obstacles.

Teams were chosen by the gang's time-honoured methods.

And pity any unsuspecting motorist who left a car – there weren't many, right enough – in Viewforth Place during any of these games.

The least damage to vehicles would be the numerous black imprints where a ball had thudded against them.

An average of two tenement windows suffered each week.

Sunday marathon football matches were really something.

These started at 9.30am and continued until well after teatime.

The gang members went, in relays, to their various churches so that, though the sides were temporarily reduced, the game was never stopped.

Dinner and tea were eaten at staggered intervals, to keep the ball rolling.

The scorelines reached astronomical heights, like 186–185.

Afterwards, rather than "go in, and be kept in", some 20 grubby-youngsters would plague the life out of Louis Boni for free glasses of water – how patient he must have been – the gang usually got them.

Saturday, during school terms, was the day of days.

In mid-morning the gang members received their weekly bob, having had to "go the messages", break kindlers and carry in coal to earn it.

Then, in high glee, they made for John MacLeod's and Willie Kennedy's for a "barra Raisin Block' or a "barra chocolate toffee".

Thus provided, they crossed the road for the special matinee performance at the pictures.

Inevitably it would be a cowboy or gangster film, followed by the current serial.

Raucous shouts urged on the Goodies and loudly booed the Baddies ("Look out, he's behind you!").

All the while, private little fights were conducted in the semi-darkness against the Village Gang, the Alma Road Gang and the Lundavra Gang, who all had their allocated, jealously guarded seating

arrangements at the Playhouse.

Slings and water pistols were used with telling accuracy.

Immediately after the pictures, the various scenes were re-enacted by the Viewforth Gang, toting toy six-shooters and rubber knives.

Running fights took place across the roofs of MacLennan's corrugated iron store sheds.

At the rear of Sydie's, in Cinema Lane, there stood, among ladders and paint drums, the wheelless, roofless shell of a Model T Ford.

Many a thrilling "chase" took place aboard the old Tin Lizzie, as

Clearing the site of the Playhouse Cinema. Looking at side door of The Volunteer towards Cameron Square.

a dozen of the gang, making all the requisite engine and gear change noises "pursued" the luckless baddies.

Cuts and bruises were commonplace in Viewforth, as gang members fell out of trees, tumbled down a roof, or a Rhone pipe was pulled off the wall with one of them still clinging to it.

There wasn't one of the gang who didn't spend a few weeks' cooling off period in the Old Belford as a result of some hair-raising, daredevil stunt – that went wrong!

Before the lorry

Class 2B, Fort William Senior Secondary School, 1959/60
Teacher: May Macintyre
Back: Mary MacIntosh, Dorothy Campbell, Mary ?, Duncanina Macintyre, ?, Pat Argue, Roslyn Curran,
Dorothy Molloy, Phyllis MacDonald, Peter McDermid.
Middle: Ronald Young, Ewen Campbell, John Munro, Aeneas McCallum, ?, Andrew Paterson, John Wilson, Angus McInnes, ?.
Front: Edward Boyle, Angus MacDonald, Iain Morrison, ?, Donald Munro, Jimmy Logan, Robert McKinnon, Ian Forsyth.

HOW WE WERE

Life In The High Street – Late 1940s Onwards

Life in Fort William High Street was very enjoyable. On a Saturday afternoon 'the girls' walked along one side of the High Street and 'the boys' walked along the other side, usually ending up having hot orange in Pertucci's Ice Cream Café at the Parade (where Nevisport is presently situated). Sometimes we adjourned to Faccenda's Ice Cream Café further along the High Street where we had ice cream and a fruit sauce (this usually in the Summer months). We felt very grown-up doing this!

At that time, there was a Teenagers' Club who met every Wednesday night in Fraser's Café to dance, usually to the music provided by the late Mr John Brown who had a splendid collection of gramophone records.

Mr Brown also provided the music for the school dances, held in the gymnasium in Fort William Secondary School but I recall a Christmas dance once being held in the Masonic Club in the High Street, though I cannot recall the band on that occasion. Sometimes we had Friday night dances in Fraser's Café and especially at Christmas time, decorations, a tree was decorated and a great time was had by all.

Also in the 1950s there were Friday night dances in K.K. Cameron's Café in the West End and the late Billy Corrigan was responsible for taking tickets at the door. The band at some of these dances was The Blue Stars.

In the summer months, we played tennis on the courts in Achintore Road where there now stand two handsome houses, and in the winter months we played badminton in the Drill Hall opposite St Mary's Church.

We also cycled a lot, went for walks up Glen Nevis, along the Canal Banks at Banavie. Always turning homewards to Fort William.

In the Autumn and Winter months, the Farmers' Dance and Police Dance were held in the Highland Hotel and Peter MacLennan's Staff Dance, MacBrayne's Staff Dance and the B.A. Staff Dance were held in the Grand Hotel, Gordon Square. The dress to these dances was very much long evening dresses for the ladies and dinner-suits or Highland evening wear for the gents.

There were also dances held, from time to time, in the Town Hall, Cameron Square, now no longer there.

Going to the Pictures was a great pastime, especially in the winter months, to the Playhouse Cinema opposite Cameron Square. There was a morning film for young school children, afternoon show and the "late" show was 7.45 p.m. – 10.15 p.m. approx.

There were Scottish Country Dance classes held in the Masonic Hall, one of the instructors being the late Mary MacPherson.

Life seemed a lot more simple then and Fort William was a small town, where it seemed to be that people looked out for one another.

Another great pastime was keeping in touch with the 6-Day Motor Bike Trials, racing from school to watch the riders negotiate the rocky brae!

Alexandra Hotel

Duncansburgh Church

Duncansburgh Church Manse

Parade House

Behind parade house,
    Mamore Cottage family home
    of the Macdougall family

Episcopal Church

Bank Street – Top Of Bank
    Street, Hydro-Board
    Showroom & Office

Maccabe & Macarthur, fruit &
    veg. shop

John Macleod, Stationers

Sydie, Painters & Decorators

Macdonald & Forbes,
    Family Butchers

Commercial Hotel

Archway to Viewforth,
    flatted tenement property
    – now car park

Fraser, House Furnishers

Peter MacLennan's, Outfitters,
    Tailors, Family Grocery

W. Kennedy, Stationer

British Linen Bank
    – on floor above bank,
    Robert Dow, Solicitor

Town Hall

Memories of shop/business names – 1948 onwards

Jaz. Mackenzie, Registrar

F.P. Church

West Highland Museum

R. Riddler, Licensed Grocer

H. Mackenzie, Tweeds &
    Knitwear

A. Macdonald, Outfitter

Lipton, Grocers

Lawrie Blair, Fishmonger.
    There was an open-fronted
    shop with a marble display
    area for fish, etc.

Donald (Dancer) Cameron,
    Fish & Chip Shop

Geddes's, Ladies' Clothes and
    Household Articles.

Joe Faccenda's,
    Ice Cream Shop.

O.B. Ross, shoe shop

Munro, Butchers.

Fraser's Café

Macdonald Bros.
    Licensed Grocers

Hume's, Stationers

Grand Hotel

Gordon Square
    – Macrae & Dick, Taxis,
    Car Repair Shop, Petrol

Railway Station – and the
    hearse was garaged there.
    The hearse drivers were the
    late Hughie Macneil and the
    late Hughie Carr.

Macintyre's Garage

Court House & Police Station

West End Hotel

Lundavra Road

Greenhill Boys' Hostel

Fort William Primary &
    Secondary School and
    headmaster's house

The Slaughter House used to

be where Belhaven Ward now stands and the Auction Mart was at Nevis Bridge where there is now a tartan & knitwear business with restaurant facilities.

Opposite Alexandra Hotel –

Parade Garage, owned (I think) by the late Joe Macpherson

Pertucci's Ice Cream Shop

Clyne, Tailors

Co-Op Drapery, Grocery & Butcher

Esso Petroleum Co., Petrol storage tanks & office, was situated at Tweedale but amalgamated with Shell in the position Scottish Fuels now occupies. Esso and Shell shared facilities from early in 1940.

Tweedale flats.

Marshall & Pearson's – petrol pumps, repair garage and where the ambulance was garaged

Imperial Hotel

Argyll Bar

MacEwen's, Grocer's

Kean's, Chemist

MacGillivray, Grocer

Masonic Hall

Shoe Shop (cannot remember the name)

Lachie Wynne, Butchers

J. Mackay, Jeweller

Palace Hotel

Mairi MacIntyre, tweeds & tartans with knitwear

Willie Fraser, Car Repairs

Volunteer Bar

Playhouse Cinema

Mary Downie, Lingerie (there was a newsagent Angus Kennedy nearby)

M.& M. Gordon, Lending Library, Wireless Batteries, Torches

P. Robertson, Ironmongers

Macmaster's, Fruit & Veg.

Cooper's, Grocers

Duncan Macintyre, Butcher

Marion Weir, Music Shop

Fraser's, Hairdressers

Station Hotel

Willie Watt had a small fresh fish van at the entrance to the station

MacBrayne's Buses and Repair Shop with office

accommodation. The manager lived in the flat above – the late John Clark

R. Macdonald, Hairdresser

Campbell Macpherson, Optician

K.K. Cameron, Bakers & Function Room.

M. Macintyre, Gift Shop.

Flatted property along the High Street finishing almost opposite the West End Hotel.

Reference is made in the text to well known figures in Fort William who are no longer with us – and I trust that this does not upset any relative. I wish to apologise for any distress caused.

The order of the shop name list is most likely not in correct order - just names remembered.

(Mrs) Anne M. Taylor (Née Kennedy)

Our Memory Years

Our period is from the '40s to the late '70s. When TV was in its infancy. No microwaves. Few houses had telephones, and those that did took messages for their neighbours. Many houses still cooked with the coal fired ranges. We did have a wide variety of shops – which covered all our needs.

O.B. Ross's. How many of you can recall how grown-up you felt when you could afford your first pair of high heels. Yes, there were three other shoe outlets, but O.B.'s was the ultimate.

Alistair MacDonald's.

Geddes's.

MacLennan's for every clothing need.

Mary Downie's for fancy underwear and nightwear – where you spent more than you meant to, just so Miss Downie wouldn't think you couldn't afford her prices. I'm sure there's a few reading this know what I mean.

Marion Weir's. Her shop was an Aladdin's cave, and yet she knew exactly where everything was. Piles of records – one on top of the other – hardly any room to turn, and yet you always came out with what you wanted.

MacDonald Brothers, where the dairy products, large blocks of butter and cheese were kept on marble slabs behind the serving area, and where the assistants must have walked miles each day, as almost every request needed a walk to the back shop.

Mary & Margaret Gordon's Music and Record Shop, where you could also join their lending library. This was where we went to take out romances, as Miss Stewart – who ran the Burgh Library – would not allow youngsters to take out 'love stories', but for a few pence we could indulge at Gordons Lending Library (and no censorship).

R.S.MacColl's. After the rationing of the post-war years, it was a dream come true the day sweets came off the rationing. The queues along the High Street were evidence of such an eventful day for so many youngsters.

Faccenda's – Ice Creams and Teas. This was run by Joe Faccenda and family. First Class Ice Cream, made on the premises. Joe Faccenda was the first premises in Lochaber to have a Juke Box, and to sit there with a coffee, and listen to music that was 'our music' was just 'so grown-up'. Joe enjoyed the company of youngsters, but our music used to grate on Mrs Faccenda, and often she switched the Juke Box off.

Hugh Cameron, Coal Merchant. This office in Monzie Square, behind the Bank of Scotland, was where people ordered and paid for their coal orders. Manager was Alistair MacDougall, a real gentleman, and the office was run by Mrs Collier and Mya Black, and clerks Mary Kennedy and Mary Donaldson. It was the one office in town where there was always a huge coal fire burning. Coal was Graded from 1 to 7, and you bought what you could afford. (usually Grade 3) and this was 7/6d. a bag . Deliveries every week, with country customers buying 2 or 3 tons at a time. Coalmen were many and varied, but the mainstay was Jock Petrie and his sons.

MacPherson, Opticians. This new build at top of Station Brae, was run by Campbell MacPherson, a very pleasant optician, who had his display room downstairs and consulting rooms upstairs.

These premises were later used by Cargill's Dairy, and Fitzsimmons the Electricians.

K.K. Cameron's. We have asked so many people of their memories of K.K.'s, and almost without exception the first and abiding memory is 'the smell of the morning rolls'. Nobody makes them like that anymore! (Thanks to Jim Wallace and his crew we can keep that sense of smell as a childhood memory). Whether as a schoolchild on the way to school buying a play piece, or a busy Mum needing something for the family dinner, KK's was a port of call for us all. And K.K. vans around our roads and villages were

a familiar sight. Drivers – Colin Cameron (Colibus) and Tommy Disher. Restaurant at the rear of the shop was always packed in summer, and waitresses in neat black dresses and white aprons attended to us no matter how busy they were – they never flapped.

Mary MacIntyre – (Mary Moik's). Catered for so many tastes. Ladies Lingerie, Linen, Fancy Goods, etc. This was one shop where you could browse, before that became fashionable. "No hurry, have a good look around" was the byword. Miss MacIntyre was ably assisted by Mary MacHugh and Lucy MacInnes.

The Town Hall

This was the hub of the town, and every meeting or concert of any worth was held here, as well as regular weekly dances. We had many artistes of note – the White Heather Club where many of our young Scottish entertainers began their Show Biz

careers, Calum Kennedy, Alistair Gilles, the Alexander Brothers, Wilfred Pickles, Whists, Ceilidhs, Amateur Dramatics, Pantomimes, and much much more.

One event guaranteed to fill the Hall was the 'Greeting Meetings'! This was the Rate Payers meeting – prior to the Town Council elections, where those seeking

re-election and those standing for election would answer questions from the public, generally about what had been done (or not done) in the previous term of office. This generated many instances of Highland humour, some very droll remarks, and much letting off steam. Usually speakers were encouraged by the audience.

Poetry — by Joe Robson

The Pelmet
I'm a Bobby in Fort William, and the High Street is my Beat,
You can't beat it for variety, though it's gie sair on the feet,
I met a poor wee lad one day, crying as if he'd die,
I dried his tears and asked him – what was wrong to make him cry.

He said "I've lost my Mummy, when she hurried out that shop,
I dinnae think she heard me, when I shouted her to stop
I said "I hope you've learnt a lesson – even if I'm the one to teach it.
Next time – Hang on to her skirt." Said he, " I couldna reach it"!!!

Affa Dear!
Inside the door of Scottish Crafts, a pile of antlers lay.
Looking at the price – an Aberdonian was heard to say,
"They're affa dear, are they no?" His mate said, "No, they're cheap."
"Of course they're affa deer, did you think they're affa sheep!"

Santa's Reindeer
The team that pulls Old Santa's sledge
Are strong and without fear,
The leader is a fine big stag – Rudolph the red-nosed deer.
Bruno the brown-nosed deer comes last.
Why he's called that has him quaking.
He can run as fast as all the rest
But he's not so good at braking!!!

Note McCabe's Fruit Shop

The Playhouse – Bingo Days!

Joyce Vickers

The Playhouse in the High Street was a Mecca for everyone in its time. When TV took over in most homes, C.A.C. (Caledonian Associated Cinemas) decided to have Bingo in the Playhouse, three times a week, and it certainly took off.

Joyce was the third 'caller' following George Mileham, and Keith Barlow. People became friends and regulars and when she took her seat at the bingo machine up on stage, a glance along the rows told her if anyone was missing. If they were, enquiries were made and if it was illness, loss of a loved one, or an accident, a card and often flowers would be sent to the home of that person.

It was not only a Bingo Hall, but a venue for everyone to get together for a night out and a blether. Nettie did the teas and hot-dogs at half-time, and for those who liked a 'wee dram' at half-

time they would find their drinks all ready poured for them in the Volunteer Bar next door – complete with a coal fire in the winter.

Bingo players have always been generous and any worthwhile cause was contributed to with open hearts and hands. A bucket was handed along the rows of seats and very heavy it became by the time it reached the bottom rows.

I have warm and wonderful memories of my time as a caller in the 'Picturehouse Bingo'. Sandy Stewart preceded Ben Hughes as manager, Donnie

Nicholson checked the winning books, Cathy who switched on the lights as each number was called, and Molly and Grace who sold the books and counted out all the winning monies. Also, all the school lads and lasses who ran up and down the aisles and lowered the 'buckets on a string' down from the balcony, with the book of any winner in that area.

Happy Days!

Donnie Nicholson, Christine MacLeod, Sally Findlay, Neil MacLeod, Grace Brooks, Nettie MacBeth, Cathy MacPhee

The Auction Mart, Nevis Bridge

The Auction Mart was demolished in 1967. Built by Angus Cameron in 1896, it was known locally as the Ben Nevis Mart until 1926 when a body of local farmers took shares in it and called the Company 'Lochaber Farmers Livestock Mart'. It continued to be run by Angus Cameron until 1934 when his son Donald, who farmed Achintee took over.

The older generation can remember the many sales held in the Mart, and how, just before a sale, the fields where Claggan houses now stand would be full of cattle.

In the days before electricity, buyers were provided with candles when a large sale was on and, if it became dark before the sale was finished, they would use these to inspect the animal in the ring.

The one great fault with this mart was its distance from the Railway Loading bank, which meant that the animals had to be driven half a mile to Fort William. This was a nightmare to householders on the route, but a great joy to the local boys, who earned sixpences for retrieving runaway animals. On one occasion a bullock being chased by a boy ran into the Alexandra Hotel and all around the dining room where the guests were at dinner. Another time a cow went missing after it had dashed down the High Street. It was later found in an upstairs bedroom in Cochrane's Hotel!   ✧

HOUSING

Not for most of us the luxury of walking into a house of our own. Married life usually started off 'in rooms'. sometimes with in-laws, but mostly with an older person – widow or widower – who had a spare room in their house. Average time to wait for a house was two and a half years. How many of you started off in rooms? How many of you were happy – but not thrilled – to get a house on New Pier Terrace, and took it knowing that the next step was a council house of your own? Who can remember where Ben Nevis Terrace and Ben Nevis Buildings were? All temporary housing. Time in rooms gave young couples a learning curve – if you didn't know how to do something, parents helped or the person whose house you were in. Perhaps it's wrong to pass comment, but it seems that now social workers and the new term – project workers – take that place in the community. And the closeness of community life is gone.

We accepted that we had to wait for a house. It gave you time to prepare. Although a room was fine when it was just two of you, when children came along it could be very difficult trying to live in one room and to cope with a baby or young toddler. But we did it – and we managed to survive.   ✧

HIGH STREET, FORT WILLIAM.

Station Square from the Pier, Fort William   33960

Armadale Buildings

The young boys of Fort William, born and living their early lives during the period of some twenty years between the two world wars fell broadly into two categories – those who were going to be old enough to participate actively in the coming conflict and those who would be young enough to serve in the Forces, after the War was over

For all of us, however, the early period was a happy one of relative oblivion to the growing dark clouds of war. One of the reasons for this was probably the fact that we were not constantly exposed to the 'media' – since most people did not have radios and TV had not been heard of. Few people had in fact ever travelled more than 50 or 100 miles from Fort William.

A weekly visit to the cinema provided all the International news through 'Movietone News' and suchlike programmes supporting the main feature film.

There were only two schools – St Mary's and Achintore. St Mary's was a Primary School only and Achintore School a combined Primary and Secondary school for a very large area, including pupils from some of the Inner Hebrides. There was a Primary School at Inverlochy, but strictly speaking, this was outside the Town boundary. We all came together finally in the Secondary School at Achintore and there was never any question of sectarianism – which speaks for itself of the good and happy relationship that the townspeople enjoyed. It speaks further of the size of the population that all children over 12 could be accommodated in what now appears to be a very small building.

With the outbreak of war additional facilities had to be found as the school rolls were expanding by city evacuees and by the families of military and particularly naval personnel. St Andrew's Church Hall was one such extension.

Life for the children of Fort William tended to follow a pattern of seasons.

Winter – Sledging on the Golf Course above the Highland Hotel, watching curling on the ponds at the entrance to Glen Nevis (sometimes skating on them if the grown-ups weren't around). Long frosts and heavy snowfalls were much more common than they are now.

Spring – The March burning of the Cow Hill where all the boys, with home-made beaters, controlled the long lines of flaming heather and winter dried grass.

Summer – Summer was for swimming at various locations on the River Nevis and one's ability dictated where you swam, as some sites were more dangerous than others – though this was partially overcome as the older boys were very good at keeping an eye on the younger ones. There was, of course, no indoor swimming pool at that time. Fire seemed to hold a fascination for us and we spent a lot of time lighting fires and using them to boil rowan berries, to melt and cast lead into various shapes, and to roast potatoes which served very well in place of rationed sweets.

Autumn – The chestnut trees were in full fruit and much time and effort was spent in collecting 'bullies' or throwing sticks into the trees to try to knock them down. Every boy had a string of these pierced conkers from which to select his next armour-plated 'all-winning' conker.

Armadale Buildings

The environs of this area provided some very entertaining places, and our base was the garage at Valtos, home of Dr MacIver. The kindly doctor allowed us to use his garage as a kind of gang hut – which we did, despite that it was often cluttered with peats and potatoes, etc., being payments in kind delivered to the doctor. People were poorer then, and there was no National Health Service. In the same way, sometimes a grouse or other local wildlife would find

it's way to the good Doctor's table, often in his SS Jaguar car, a wondrous vehicle for its time. We would periodically be taken on his country rounds, visiting places like Onich, Spean Bridge, etc. During these runs, the good doctor would recount tales of the Great World War or, best of all, stories about the excavations in Mesopotamia and Egypt which interested him

Behind the Doctor's garage was the workshop of Mr MacNicoll, a very gentle old man who allowed us to watch him carry out his trade.

The Co-op Butchers

As the horse and cart was still the primary means of transport Mr MacNicoll was often called upon to repair of make cart wheels and very impressive work it was. Great masses of shavings would accumulate on the workshop floor, and if we swept them up and generally tidied them up we were allowed to use some of the tools and spare pieces of wood to make whatever took our fancy. When the wooden wheels had been completed we often followed them across to the nearby Blacksmith's shop where the two Jockys would select long flat lengths of iron, measure them carefully, and shape them to the required diameter, which was always a fraction less than the wooden wheel.

By turning the huge iron rings in the smiddy fire the iron expanded to fit most neatly over the wheels. Smoke poured from the wheel as the red hot iron rim was hammered on over the wooden wheel and the whole thing plunged in a tub of cold water to shrink the tyre firmly in place. Because of the intense heat needed for most of the work in the smiddy, there was a lot of bellows pumping to be done and the reward for this task was being allowed to make mini horse shoes or throw iron filings on the fire, which would result in a glorious volcano of bright sparkling flame. Some years later I made my first ice axe there, although on reflection, it would have been better left to Jocky despite our youthful apprenticeship.

Near the smiddy is the Craigs Rock from behind which, as from the Sugar Loaf, the gunners of the Bonnie Prince fired unsuccessfully upon the Fort in 1745. With little chisels , made in the smiddy, we spent much of our time trying to demolish the rock – with an outcome similar to that of the gunners – unsuccessful! The Craigs Rock provided us with many daring – if short – climbs. Beyond the rock is the Craigs Cemetery, still very much in use

The Parade

at that time but never properly tended. Whins and long grass grew profusely and provided an ideal range for Cowboys and Indians. When the grass was crisp and dry like that on the Cow Hill, in Spring we fired it, and we never got into trouble for doing so. One can only conclude that we were carrying out some public service. Within a very short time the new grass burst forth and the cemetery appeared fresh and well cared for. During burials we always stopped playing and watched from a respectful distance.

Life and Death seemed so much closer at hand as modern medical treatments – especially antibiotics – lay some time in the future. On the far side of the graveyard lay the Poorhouse and the Slaughterhouse. The latter used by local butchers who bought and processed their own livestock. We often made our way there as behind the slaughterhouse lay a huger long-barrelled field gun from the WW1. When tired of sitting on the iron gun layers, chairs, and spinning the wheels which lowered or increased the range, we would stand at the open door of the slaughterhouse while various animals were being dispatched. It all seemed such a part of life to us that it never made us callous towards animals. In fact, the lamb given to Father Thomas Wynne when he was very small was fondly taken care of by us all and followed the young Thomas everywhere including visits to St. Mary's School where it would wag its tail when he re-appeared. After a time, the lamb's forays into the gardens of the adjoining Convent incurred the wrath of the gardener, and it had to be sent to pastures new. The Kennedys at Achriach took it in hand and in due course, Kirri as it was called, produced lambs of its own over several seasons. All the shearings were collected and finally handed back – Father Thomas says his first suit was made from this fleece.

The Auction Mart

At Nevis Bridge lay the Auction Mart, which was a great source of pleasure, as one could sit high up on the raised bank of benches surrounding the ring and watch the Auctioneer, the Crofters and the Farmers bidding. Not least were the animals themselves for occasionally they were not so easily coaxed to show themselves off in the ring, and produced an additional excitement. Perhaps the greatest thrill of all was the herding of sheep and cattle at the end of the sales from the Mart to the Railway Cattle Bank which was situated to the east of the Parade Putting Green. Small boys were sent out ahead of the animals to block off the side roads, the Craigs, the open gardens, etc.in order to prevent runaways. From time to time this was not fully effective and a magnificent chase would follow the recalcitrant bullock or sheep up Victoria Road or round the Town Bowling Green.

Annual Events

Scottish Six Days Trials – we all watched from the safety of the Rocky Brae walls.

Highland Games Day in the King George V Park was especially fun as there was bunting about the town and many stalls and shows, and the Pipe Band was always a feature of this event.

Ben Nevis Race Day which originally started from the Post Office in the High Street across from the Ben Nevis Bar.   ✧

Keith Hamilton, Postman.

Note Alistair MacDonald, Drapers.

Oor Ain Kirk Bell

Contributed by Mrs. B. Jeffrey.

Whar Nevis crags wi' pride look doon, On what was once a Burgh toon
There stands a Kirk up on the brae, And it's been there for many a day.

For long the bell has tolled its message, To young and old alike
To come and join in worship, And wi' other folk unite.

To praise the Lord wi' singing, And to bow our heads in prayer
Wi' words of true thanksgiving For all we freely share.

Throughout the years of war and peace, In times of sadness and of loss
The age-old story did not cease, How Jesus died upon the cross.

He died that we might be forgiven, And his life so gladly gave
And yet he walks and talks with us, And he has the power to save.

That Kirk is here with us today, And still the bell rings ou
Accept its invitation Come inside and don't be left out.

I sit there on Sunday morning – And the flowers I admire
I enjoy the organ, music, And the singing of the Choir.

I watch the elder enter, And then with sombre look
He quietly stands in reverence, When he had op'ed the Holy Book.

The children too I like to see, And I watch their faces glow
When the minister asks a question, And they – the answer know.

I listen to the 'word of God', And I try to understand
That as I live from day to day – The Lord is in command.

I'm really glad that Kirk is here, And that I can step within
To receive a humble Blessing – And forgiveness from my sins.

For that Kirk has got a purpose, To join us in our faith
And to learn to love each other – That's what our Master saith.

I hear his voice in every chime, He speaks to every age and every clime
In joy or sorrow – peace or strife – "I am the Way – the Truth – the Life".

Side entrance to Marshall & Pearson Garage
Ex-Provost Duncan Grant, Mr Alexander, Corrie Sutherland, Angus White (Imperial Hotel),
Hector Kennedy, ?, ?, ?, Ex-Provost Donald (Danger) Cameron, ?, ?.

Kitchen Cupboard Remedies

Does this bring back memories?

Tummy Ache – Castor Oil or Syrup of Figs.

Toothache – Hot Cloth to the cheeks, or a mouthful of whisky – to be held there as long as you could hold it – without swallowing.

Constipation – Cascara.

Ear-ache – Warm olive/almond oil kept in place with cotton wool. Hot cloths tied round your ears.

Cuts –Pink lint and bandage.

Boils – Bread Poultice.

Chilblains or Hacks – Snowfire Ointment (Bright Green Concoction).

Styes in the eyes – Must be rubbed with a gold wedding ring.

To get rid of Nits – Coal Tar Soap and then hair had to combed onto paper.

To prevent getting Nits – Wash in Paraffin.

Scabies – Scrubbed hard, and gentian violet put on.

T.B. – taken to sanatorium and isolated from family. House had to fumigated.

Scarlet Fever / Diphtheria – same as above.

Many Mums dished out Castor Oil every week to all the family. (Needed or not!)

At MacDonald's the Hairdressers

Shinty and Football were generally the main topics of discussion at MacDonald's the Hairdressers at the Pierhead. But depending on the clientele on the premises at the time, the conversation could take many twists. On one of Jock's infrequent visits to MacDonald's, 'Doichen' MacDougall, the senior barber (some locals called him the 'head barber') seeing the great mop of unkempt hair on Jock's dome was heard to ask, "Have you brought your piece, Jock?"

During the long tonsorial operation which followed, wee Angus, son of Sandy Tosh the joiner, came in. 'Doiken' looked up from his labours long enough to mutter to Angus – "When you get home, son, tell your Dad he's not the only one who works on wood."

Stories

There was an English angler, taken out on the loch by boatman Donald. Every now and again, the English angler had a swig from a bottle of Scotch – but never the offer of a drop for Donald. During the fishing trip, being Lochaber, it rained. The English angler sought solace from his pipe to keep the midges away, but although his matches were dry, the match box was damp and wouldn't strike. Donald suggested the English angler could strike his match on Donald's tongue. 'It was so dry'!

Paddy Gainsford was an inveterate gambler, and a faithful churchgoer. During Mass one Ash Wednesday Paddy was observed to pull out the 'Noon Record' (a racing paper) from his pocket, suitably folded to fit between the pages of his missal – and have a wee study of form during the sermon. Paddy had his routine each day, calling at many of the shops and offices on his way to the bookies to ask "Anyone here having a flutter today?" Always smart, and his Irish accent still as strong as the day he left Ireland many years before

"Spring is here." This is always the comment from so many locals – to see the lovely herald of spring each year – the snowdrops in St Andrew's Churchyard. It makes us forget the wind and rain and winter days.

Hamish went to the doctor complaining of piles. All the while in the Fassifern Road surgery Hamish kept rubbing his elbow, and he continued to do so during the GP's examination, but a little gentle geographical questioning soon sorted things out.

Doctor – "Where do you come from Mr MacL…?"

Hamish proudly – "Ballachulish, Doctor."

Doctor – "I might have known, no wonder you don't' know your a… from your elbow

Life's Gentlemen. In the '50s, when the bus service was not so regular on the Lundavra run, many people had occasion to remember with gratitude Duncan Campbell, Jimmy Donaldson, and Bob

Morrison, who never passed them by without offering them 'a lift up the hill'. The hill was steeper then, and quite a climb.

A Wedding. Due to petrol rationing in war time, taxi owners were only allowed to travel a certain distance. A wedding party going to Corpach Church had to get a bus from Laggan to Spean Bridge – where they were met. Bridge was dressed in full regalia, flowers, etc.

Arriving at Banavie Locks to find the gates closed and boats sailing through, the bride had to endure countless jibes about the groom not waiting, but smiled through it all, knowing her groom would be there. An hour later, arriving at the Church only to find the groom had fainted. The groom recovered, and the wedding service went ahead. Attended reception and then caught the afternoon Glasgow train. An eventful day.

Angus MacDonald. Gus was a genial character, known by locals as The Laird of Blarmafoldach or Gus, the Pigman, who when you met him always said "I'm just away to look at the Noticeboard,

and if my name's not up I'll go and get the messages". (The Noticeboard was beside the Rod & Gun Shop where all death notices are displayed.)

MacLennan's

Round the back of MacLennan's, Calum, Hamish and Hector were moving bales of hay. The latter two stalwarts stood on the top of the six-bale high stack inside the stores. Their job was to manoeuvre the hay down to Calum. He, in his turn, loaded the bales onto a lorry. On his way out to the lorry for the umpteenth time, Calum heard an anguished cry and a couple of Gaelic expletives. Rushing back into the store-shed he saw Hector sprauchled on the floor.

"What happened?" asked Calum, as he helped his unfortunate colleague to his feet.

"Och, the gorrach so-and-so stepped on a bale that you took away five minutes ago!" was Hamish's scathing reply.

Royal Bank of Scotland staff

Mary (Black) Johnson, Mairi Fraser, Margaret Lamond, Sheila Mackenzie, Celia Muir, Durness Simpson, Lynette MacIntyre, Sally Hutchings, Joan Black, Jan Galloway, Florabelle Frazer

Outings

Many firms organised away days for their staff, usually consisting of a coach trip, lunch, shopping, dinner & theatre, and run on the shop holidays of May or September. Or many joined the excursion train to Glasgow for shopping, etc. The Co-op always organised one for its members and families to Arisaig, and the beach.

Fort William always shut down on the second Monday in May and in September. There was always a special train to Glasgow, and it was what everyone had saved for once Christmas was over. Everyone went shopping – not but Fort William had good shops then – but just for the variety and the experience of the large city. No matter where you went on one of these 'away days' you always met folk from the Gearasdan. Everyone knew the High Street was closed down for the day, and it was the norm. On the journey back, we had a sing-song, we had a mannequin parade with all the 'high fashion' items bought that day, and we had a pleasant day out. It is so easy now with modern transport for everyone to 'do their own thing'. But the Community enjoying itself isn't the same.

Fort William Community Council tried to recreate the excursion train for the West Highland Line Centenary in 1996 – a one-off occasion! ✧

Cathy Bryce, Vera MacDonald, Anne Cameron, Helen McBean,
??, Dolly MacVarish, Juditha Rysnik, Mary Black.

SPORTS AND PASTIMES

Fort William Swimming Pool

There had been talk about building a swimming pool in the Fort from as far back as the thirties. In 1966 a small swimming pool was built at Lochaber High School, which was much used by the secondary pupils.

However the district council at the time felt that there was a need for a second pool given the amount of tourism in the area. Fund raising activities were started in the early '50s and '60s, including the mile of pennies campaign by local woman Betty Thompson. One of the sites discussed for the new swimming pool was at Ashburn Lane. However, in 1974 the dream of a municipal pool came to fruition when, despite much

criticism about where it was sited, a modern Olympic size facility was built on the town park. A new town park was built at Claggan with an excellent pavilion and grandstand The swimming pool was the flagship of the Highlands and a similar smaller sized facility was built in Oban that same year.

The grand opening took place on June 10th 1974 and Provost George K.B. Henderson confidently predicted that the new pool would

be greatly enjoyed by the people of Lochaber and its many visitors. Sir Donald Cameron of Lochiel planted a ceremonial tree to commemorate the event. Thirty years later he returned to plant another for the thirtieth anniversary celebrations. Another well-kent face who took part in the proceedings was Sir Jimmy Savile. Two opening events had to be held that day due to the massive crowds that attended, one at 2pm and another at 4pm. Public demonstrations were held for life-saving, water polo and synchronised swimming these were organised by David Cargill the Principal PE Teacher at Lochaber

High School. The first paying customer arrived on the morning of June 18th, straight off night shift from the Pulp and Paper mill. The cost of his swim was ten pence. Since then more then four million swimmers have used the facility.

In its first year of operation, despite attracting over 150,000 swimmers the cost of operating the new facility made the headlines in the local newspapers. District councillors were told that in order to cut down on expenditure, the number of staff would have to be cut. There were twenty-two staff employed at the facility many of whom had come into the area for their job at the pool. It was also of much concern that there was nobody capable of teaching swimming. The following year the press reported a different picture the pool was "bursting at the seams" which gave the confidence that the facility would not end up a municipal white elephant. Also, a matter for modest concern was reported to the council by the manager about the amount of foreign visitors who had the habit of wandering about in the altogether.

The first official swimming club was formed in 1974 and within five years swimmers were competing and winning medals at the National championships. The annual Loch Linnhe swim was restarted that year and nine competitors braved the elements. On a wet and windy day, a strong current dragged all but one competitor into the estuary of the river Lochy.. The annual Christmas galas were outstandingly successful and indeed on one occasion the police had to be called out to control the crowds.

In 1982, the pool hosted the North of Scotland swimming championships where the local club won thirty-two gold medals and the following year the pool had a visit from Olympic champion David Wilkie who presented autographed certificates to young swimmers. The Fort William swimming pool was renamed in 1987, following extensive renovations and the now Lochaber Leisure Centre is one of Highland Council,s showpiece facilities with the swimming pool being the busiest council operated pool in the Highlands.   ✦

The Garrison Theatre

This was in the Parade area, in front of Parade House and originally for the use of the troops stationed here during the war years, afterwards it became for the use of the locals. Many ENSA shows were held in it, and enjoyed by all. But you had to be invited in by a member of the forces.

Also, before each school in the town area got their own canteen – meals were provided here and the children marched from school to the Garrison every lunchtime. One day soup and a main course, next day main course and pudding, and custard was poured out of a huge jug (some days thick and some days thin & watery) it depended on who made it or how long it had been standing.   ✧

Nicknames

As we all know names have given to people for many reasons, some are easily worked out, but many more – we would love to get explanations for.

From my own little patch at Lundavra came such names as Annie Woodbine, Scarce of Hair, Gleneagles, Beezer, Mrs Spragg, Mrs Cookie, Lugs, and I have often wondered how they got their names. Some are obvious, but others? Scooty Watson, Speed Gibson, Skeesh Gillies.   ✧

What did we do?

Shinty

Each area in Lochaber had a strong team, some rivalry between them all. Some terrific shinty players. Some with their own peculiarities – such as Doxie Cameron who always wore gloves but only the left hand glove. The right hand glove was always abandoned.

Cricket

Fort William cricket team often played in matches against Fort Augustus Abbey in the 50's.

There was also a B.A. Team – stalwarts Fred Andrews, Jack Llewellyn, Vic Pratt, Fred White, and the joker of the team Paddy Atkinson.

Matches were played locally and in Oban.

Football

Dreams of 'winning the coupon' kept us hoping all week, just as the Lottery does now for so many people. Main coupons were Littlewood's and Vernon's.

A sheet containing the football results was available in Willie Kennedy the Newsagents at 5.00pm on a Saturday evening – no TV or Teletext for the scores then!

Lochaber Wheelers

The Cycling Club that organised many trips on our bicycles. There were regular races the length of Kilmallie Road in Caol, also from Fort William to the 3 Mile Water.

Sam Horner and Richard MacFadyen were leading cyclists. ✧

Fraser, the Hairdresser

Hugh Fraser, the hairdresser, played a leading part in local sporting activities. The Loch Swim and the Ben Nevis Race were two of his favourites. The once popular Fort William Fancy Dress Parade also took up much of his time.

This establishment comprised Ladies Hairdressing, downstairs and Gent's Barbers on street level. Point of Entry was via the shop which was a Tobacconists, and the smell of all the different tobaccos, which were loose and stored in glass jars, is a childhood memory that lingers on.

The Fraser family also lived in the flats above the shop, Queen Anne Buildings.   ✧

FW Reading & Recreation Club

The YM as it was known had their premises behind MacLean's Dairy in what is now the Free Church building. A popular haunt for young and old, known by many young lads as the Billiard Hall, it consisted of two rooms, with a billiard table in each room, a good table in one, and the other, which the novices played on, known as 'the Golf Course'. This building had its lease terminated in August 1961.

The Lochaber Fiddlers rehearsing for Mrs Cameron Head's Ball at Inverailort Castle.

The Scottish Community Drama Association held its local competitions for Adults and Juniors each year in the Town Hall, with half a dozen or more local clubs competing, some entering more than one play. The SCDA is still active but sadly a shadow of its former self in Lochaber.

SCOTTISH COMMUNITY DRAMA ASSOCIATION
(Lochaber District)

SEVENTH
LOCHABER YOUTH
DRAMA FESTIVAL

In the TOWN HALL, FORT WILLIAM
On WEDNESDAY, 14th FEBRUARY, 1968

PROGRAMME

Drama Assessor :
Mrs. Nelson

PROGRAMME - 6d

GLENFINNAN DRAMATIC CLUB (JUNIORS) TEAM 'B'

present

"THE PIE AND THE TART"
Adapted from the French by Hugh Chesterman

CAST

Pierre) Vagabonds	.. ..	Joseph Gillies
Jean)	.. ..	.. Jim Cameron
Gaspard Gaultier	.. .. ..	Alick Gillies
Marion, his wife	.. .. ..	.. Rosemary Gillies

Scene - Outside cake shop in Paris.
Period - Fifteenth century.
Producer - A.M. Templeton.
Stage Manager - Angus Macdonald.

Properties and costumes made by Club.

* * * *

FORT WILLIAM AMATEUR DRAMATIC SOCIETY (JUNIOR SECTION)

present

"PADDLY POOLS"
by Miles Malleson

CAST

Grandpa	.. ..	..Charles Ross
Tony	.. ..	Alan Davidson
His Three Friends	.. .. ..	1. Charles Stewart
		2. Alison Smith
		3. Yasmin Sulamain
The Soul of the Short Green Grass	.. ..	Pat Reid
The Soul of the Wild Flowers	..	..Helen McConville
The Soul of the Trees	.. ..	Rietta Sulamain
The Soul of All the Rabbits	..	Marie MacNeil
The Spirits of the Sunset		..Barbara MacKenzie

Kathleen MacNeil, Aileen Davidson,
Jacqueline MacAndrew, Jeanne Sulamain,
Evelyn Roe, Teresa Murphy, Christine Grace

Scene - (a) In the Woods. (b) On the Other Side.
(c) as (a).
Period - 1940 - '45.
Producer - M. Richmond Jamieson.

All scenery, properties and costumes made by Club.

GLENFINNAN DRAMATIC CLUB (JUNIORS) TEAM 'A'

present

"RORY AFORESAID"
by John Brandane

CAST

MacConnachie, the Court Officer	.. Angus Gillies
Duncan MacCallum, Merchant and	
Sheep Farmer at Ardnish	... .. Ian Blyth
Rory MacColl, Shepherd to MacCallum	..Hugh Cameron
Mr. MacIntosh, an Oban Lawyer..	.. Arthur Gillies
The Sheriff-Substitute	.. .. Gordon Macdonald
Mrs. MacLean, a Crofter Widow Woman	..Anne Cameron
Members of the Public	.. .. ..Joan Gillies
	.. .. .. Maureen Gillies
	.. .. .. Mary Gillies
	.. .. .. Alistair Gillies

Scene - Court Room in a West Highland Town.
Period - Present.
Producer - A.M. Templeton.
Stage Manager - Angus Macdonald.

* * * *

The Old Library, Bank Street

Don McGavin

I was brought down from Sutherland to be the Divisional Librarian for Lochaber, at the instigation of Councillor Walter Cameron. Originally, I was based in Caol Library, with not very much to do. Then, in their infinite wisdom, the powers that were in Inverness, through a series of reorganisations decided I should be branch librarian in Fort William.

At that time the town's library was situated in a small square, where the Citizens Advice Bureau is now. It was little more than a damp shed, with windows along one side. Next door was the shed out of which the District Council's gardeners operated. There was also in the square the WRVS office and free handout shop. In the opposite corner from the library there was the schools dentist. In the days of the old Inverness County library, the library was run by Mrs Maclaren, assisted by Mrs Thompson and a young lass called Trish. (I can't remember her second name) and was open to the public for 2-hour spells most mornings and afternoons of the week, and they had run it happily for years. Into this happy scenario

I was thrust willy nilly. One big snag – the place had absolutely no "facilities" – not good for one who drinks lots of tea! I had to be in there at 9am, to do administrative tasks (not terribly onerous) but at 10, when Mrs Mac came in, I had to run like hell through Viewforth car park to the convenience behind the ruins of the old Town Hall. And then, in their wisdom, the District Council demolished the place to make way for the new Tourist Office and cinema.

Panic! Then I reasoned that as I paid all my rates I was entitled to use the Council facilities in Lochaber House, which I did until Highland Region put a small Portakabin in the square outside the library. Such luxury! All mod cons and space to make up exchanges, etc. And so things were until the building of the existing library on the site of the old Co-op and its

famous hanging tree. Before that however. I had to look at possible sites in Fort William for the new library. MacKay's premises, ex-Presto's, was one possibility. Another was the old Bank building on the corner of Cameron Square, now MacIntyre's the estate agent, rejected on the grounds of poor disabled access.

The old library was a prime example of how little the old Inverness County cared for Lochaber and Fort William. Their standards fell far short of what I had known in Sutherland, and indeed fell short of any national standards, but all we got were promises.

If there was one good thing to come out of the old Highland Region, it was the new library in Fort William. But at least in the old one, with Mrs Mac, the "craic" was always good!

Camera Club outing 1960/70
Jimmy Batchen, Raymond Hervo, Jean Miller, Alex Gillespie, Dusty Miller, John Bowstead
Jessie Batchen, Mary Johnstone (Black), Mrs Gillespie Senior, Margaret Thompson, Peter Thompson
Jean Hervo, Mary Gillespie, Ewen Gillespie

Fort William Bowling Club

Inverlochy Concert Party

British Legion Day Out to Castle Stalker

Back: George Smith, Tony MacMillan, Colin MacPhedran, ?? Stewart, Ian McIntosh, Angus Campbell
Michael O'Shaughnesy, Hughie MacMillan, Bob McCartney, Ian Kennedy, Tommy Lyon, George Phillips.
Front: Jimmy Gordon (Bus Driver), George Dryden, Harry Stewart, Stewart MacKenzie, Billy MacLeod, Kenny MacLaren, Nat. Rodgers,
Alec MacKin, Robbie Cameron, Jacjie ????.

St Mary's Football Team.
Back: Alistair MacMillan, Roddy Annand, Vance Stewart, John Delaney (Goalie), Hugh Plunkett, Jimmy MacKinnon, Pat Kelly.
Front: Peter Nolan, Bobby Gribben, Ian MacLean, Alistair MacKinnon, Alec MacKin.

Lochaber Athletic Club Committee
Back: Alex. MacLeod, Donald MacDonald, Duncan MacIntyre, George MacPherson, Jimmy Conn.
Front: Angus Campbell, Pat Neish, A. Soutar

THOSE WERE THE DAYS IN VIEWFORTH
Part 4

Iain Abernethy
Formerly of 2 Viewforth Place

During Lochaber's summer football season the Viewforth Gang betook themselves to the Town Park to watch teams like Argyll Rovers, Inverlochy, Kilmallie, Kinlochleven United, Lochaber Wednesday and St Mary's, and to act as ball boys.

About this time, too, there was always a market for cigarette cards of footballers – of a slightly higher level than Lochaber Welfare, admittedly.

Most of the gang had first-rate collections. And they had an ingenious game involving the cards, called *Face or a Blank?*

This was played on the toss-of-a-coin principle, serving to swell some card holdings and ruin others.

Occasionally a "fair" was held in the drying green below the red brick building.

Hoop-la, darts and coconut shy winners were rewarded with purloined apples, pears and nuts.

One of the mothers added to the sense of occasion by dressing up as a gipsy and telling the fortunes of the other Viewforth mums for threepence atime.

The proceeds from this venture usually bought a new rubber football for the marathon matches.

Access to the fair was by way of the two closes and stone stairs leading from the red building – or through the vennel which connected Cinema Lane with the back greens.

As a special privilege in the summer holidays, the gang members were allowed to go out with MacLennan's and MacEwen's lorries and Leslie's van, to distant places like Achriabhach and Blarmafoldach!

The week's supplies were delivered there – and the respective trips took virtually the whole day.

Never once did the gang return without goosegogs and strawberries.

Other diversions, like raids on the hideouts, huts and shants of other gangs were commonplace.

In wintertime Fort William (New) Golf Course made an ideal sledging place, with the extra-steep sheep track providing the supreme test of courage and skill. And many a gang member managed to sledge from the fifth fairway, down past the Hydro houses, Alma Road, and Fassifern Road, down Bank Street and into the Fire Station on the other side of the High Street!

In their more cultured moments the gang found time for fishing.

They caught rockies, cuddies and flukies at the Slip, down from Marshall's Garage.

The few fish that were landed were thrust upon the three cats kept by MacLennan's storeman, Jock MacPhee (The First), in return for the freedom of the sheds where the gang's wrestling bouts were held among the hay.

Among the more enterprising activities were the manufacturing of lead knives and tomahawks – and tar marble! Chunks of lead were removed from derelict roofing, "smelted" and poured into earthen moulds. When the molten masses hardened, the gang had some realistic, weighty weapons. On hot summer's days the marbles were made from the bubbling tar in the middle of a traffic-less Fassifern Road, between St John's Hame and The Cume.

Musical and entertainment tastes, apart from Radio Luxembourg and the Playhouse – *This is a Caledonian Associated Cinema* – were centred on the Town Hall.

Many a concert and variety show was heard by a grimy audience crowded around the well of the locked side door. Eventually a hole was bored in the wood and the gang took it in turns, to watch the performances.

Came the year 1953 and most of the indigenous Viewforth families made ready to move to the new council houses in Claggan.

With their departure came the advent of Polish, Lithuanian and Ukrainian exiles to the Viewforth scene.

Variegated foreign tongues combined with the Gaelic and English of the remaining handful of original inhabitants.

A new era was opening up – and with it the end of the Viewforth Gang.   ✧

The End of an Era
Would we let it happen now? The Station, the Pier and the Bus Depot. This was a meeting place – never the same again!

Stormy Weather

WHERE WE WERE

Pipe Band in Station Square

Pavilion in Achintore Road

How many of you did your courting here? A cold place – unless you were there first and got the sheltered side away from the wind. There's a few tales to be told from here, I'm sure?

SUSPENSION BRIDGE AND BEN NEVIS.

Lochy Bridge in gentler times.

Pipers on Parade

Canal swing bridge at Moy

FRIENDLY FORT WILLIAM

Heading northwards from Glasgow to Fort William the train climbs painfully, almost arthritically, through the Grampian range. No slur on BR rolling stock for at Corrour summit it is at 1,350 feet above sea level. Yet to the urban traveller this slowness is a balm unfolding a scenic grandeur that is hypnotic.

The backdrop: saw-edged mountains, snow-capped still in April, and Ben Nevis towering at 4,406 feet. Trackside: lochs, bottomless, cold as a witch's caress; moors, especially Rannoch, spongy, soggy, where deer leap from tuft to tuft. And the perambulating cast of characters … shaggy, black-faced sheep that look as though they are modelling mobile hearthrugs.

It is so elemental that eventually six dwellings resemble a city and the good old reliable red and green MacBrayne bus appears as vital as oxygen. Perspective returns as one approaches the town of Fort William.

What a pleasure it is to call at the buffet and to receive not a special but standard welcome (they're identical!) from Mrs Betty Mackinnon and staff.

Roll call? Mrs Betty Lees, four years at Fort William, birthplace Kinlochbervie; Mrs Katie Bergin, 2 years, Moidart; Mrs Kathie Donald and Mrs Morag MacRaild both began this year. Kathie hails from South Uist, Morag from Royton, Lancs.

Betty Mackinnon and her husband who worked for BR for 29 years came to Fort William for 'threemonths and stayed'. She started in 1961 on the restaurant cars (no. 361) between F.W. and Glasgow and then transferred to the booking office – her daughter, Barry, works there now.

'The Company took the buffet over in 1964 when the tenant's lease ran out and asked me to take over,' she explained, adding: 'Kathie, you're not taking an extra lettuce leaf?'

Betty Mackinnon, Katie Bergin, Kathie Donald, Betty Lees, Morag MacRaild, with stocktaker Jim MacDonald from Glasgow.

The girls are battling with a self-imposed diet. Kathie wasn't taking an extra leaf. Unlicensed, the buffet operates from 8.0 am to 5.0 pm weekdays.

The business is steady in the winter, busy in summer. Not too busy though to miss seeing a monster in Loch Linnhe. Betty and her husband saw it '… seven humps it had … the customers witnessed it … Jack de Manio broadcast an account twice on BBC.'

How friendly are they at Fort William? One of the regulars is 'Jock' … a one-legged seagull. We saw it. 'Poor wee soul, he can't fend for himself," said Betty Mackinnon feeding him bread which she'd bought in the town going messages. A one-legged seagull! Thank goodness he didn't say: 'Aaaah, Jim, lad!' ✧

The Ocean Mist at Banavie

The Ocean Mist – This was a sea-going yacht owned by Mr Joseph Hobbs of Inverlochy Castle and the Great Glen Cattle Ranch. Usually moored off Fort William Pier, or in Camasnagaul Bay. Locals used to joke that each day they watched it to see if the 'Creamola Gang' had struck overnight – but it maintained its pristine white.

The Creamola Gang – This was made up of workers on the Great Glen Cattle Ranch, who painted every house, steading, barn and byre, and sometimes even walls, a bright custard yellow – hence the name 'Creamola Gang'. At least when you travelled the A82, you knew what belonged to Mr. Hobbs.

ROYAL VISITORS

ACKNOWLEDGEMENTS

Ian Abernethy (Roamer)
Graham Brooks
W. Campbell, Livingston, West Lothian
Jo Cowan. (Age Concern)
Ian Ferguson (Photographer)
Alan Kirk (MacTavish's Kitchens)
John Muncie (Spean Media Services)
Margaret Muncie
Jimmy Ness
N. Robertson, Wick
A.M. Taylor, Inverness
Caol Lunch Club
Residents of Victoria Court

All the Contributors of Photographs and Stories, and Memories –
each and every one of you - **Our Very Grateful Thanks to You All.**

**Finally, our Special Thanks to Mary (Donaldson) Bruce,
who, without her enthusiasm, commitment, and sheer dogged determination,
this book would never have been published. Fort William Community Council,
and the Community at large, are extremely grateful.**

Patricia Jordan – Chair, Fort William Community Council.